Perfect Day

PERFECT
DAY

AN ENTREPRENEUR'S GUIDE TO CURING
Lifestyle Deficit Disorder and Reclaiming Your Business, Your Relationships, and Your Life

COKIE BERENYI

The Entrepreneur's Perfect Day Engineer

NEW YORK

LONDON • NASHVILLE • MELBOURNE • VANCOUVER

Perfect Day

An Entrepreneur's Guide to Curing Lifestyle Deficit Disorder and Reclaiming Your Business, Your Relationships, and Your Life

© 2018 Cokie Berenyi

Published in New York, New York, by Morgan James Publishing. Morgan James is a trademark of Morgan James, LLC. www.MorganJamesPublishing.com

The Morgan James Speakers Group can bring authors to your live event. For more information or to book an event visit The Morgan James Speakers Group at www.TheMorganJamesSpeakersGroup.com.

ISBN 9781683504986 paperback
ISBN 9781683504993 eBook
Library of Congress Control Number: 2017903910

Cover Design by:
Rachel Lopez
www.r2cdesign.com

Interior Design by:
Chris Treccani
www.3dogcreative.net

In an effort to support local communities, raise awareness and funds, Morgan James Publishing donates a percentage of all book sales for the life of each book to Habitat for Humanity Peninsula and Greater Williamsburg.

Get involved today! Visit
www.MorganJamesBuilds.com

DEDICATION

Perfect Day is dedicated to Claire. Your legacy of kindness, dedication, courage, and insight lives on.

TABLE OF CONTENTS

FOREWORD

"This is our purpose: To make as meaningful as possible this life that has been bestowed upon us; to live in such a way that we may be proud of ourselves; to act in such a way that some part of us lives on."
– OSWALD SENGLER, HISTORIAN/PHILOSOPHER

For most people, the phrase "money talks" means wealth is power. The more you have, the easier and better your life becomes. To a certain extent, it can be true; money does solve many of life's problems, but there is more to it than that. Sometimes money lies. Money says: "Make the quest for me the most important thing in your life, and I will reward you with whatever you want."

Money may tell us that if we sacrifice our time and energy, or even friends, family, and health, money will reward us for putting it first. How many people do you know who make the accumulation of money their priority, thinking that it will lead to happiness, peace of mind and great relationships?

Rarely in life is money a place of genuine freedom, joy, or clarity; yet, we routinely allow it to dictate the terms of our lives and often to be the single most important factor in the decisions we make about work, love, family and friendship.

Over the past 40+ years I have had the opportunity to counsel with and learn from some of America's happiest individuals and families. When I first started working with entrepreneurial families, we were focused on the money. One: How can I help you become financially secure and Two: How can I help you successfully transition your financial assets into future generations—a daunting task if you believe the statistics which say that less than 4% of family wealth survives three generations regardless of the planning that is done.

I was frustrated. I began asking new questions. "What is my stewardship to my wealth and when does it end?" "Is this all there is?" "What can I do to bring more peace and meaningfulness into my life and into the life of my family and loved ones... and to my clients?"

From these questions emerged Empowered Wealth® and the Empowered Wealth Mindset® and has inspired a passionate, life long quest to empower leaders in families, in businesses and in communities. This quest has led me to work with incredible leaders around the world.

Cokie Berenyi, traveling a parallel path of understanding True Wealth, has a unique ability to take complex issues and simplify them in a way so that you, the reader, regardless of your sophistication and level of success, can not only grasp concepts for accelerating your own growth and happiness, but actually have the stepping stones to follow.

I consider the insight from this book a gift that all of us need. I commend it to you. It is important for you, those you love, and all others you influence, and to the world. I am a great believer that all progress begins with motion—even the smallest step we can take each day that moves us closer to the Perfect Day will lead us ultimately to a more perfect life.

As you absorb and put into practice the concepts and tools outlined in *Perfect Day*, you will be on your way to achieving "success" as defined by one of my mentors, the great and highly admired coach John Wooden:

> *"Success is the peace of mind that comes from the self-assurance of knowing you have done your best to become the very best you are capable of becoming."*

Perfect Day will help guide you to that success.
--Lee Brower

Chief Inspirational Officer and Founder,
Empowered Wealth, LLC*
Featured teacher in the blockbuster
movie and book, *The Secret*.

*Empowered Wealth is a global leader in optimizing Gratitude, Leadership and True Wealth

INTRODUCTION
How I Woke Up

||||||||||||||||||||||||||||||

When I was growing up, the highest aspiration for a professional was to have a cushy corporate job, get a corner office, have an expense account, and—after climbing the ladder to its highest rungs—retire.

The world has changed a lot since then. Today, the notion of success is embodied in the idea of being an entrepreneur—being your own boss. The entrepreneur is the 21st century's cowboy. You are daring and fearless. You are a pioneer and innovator, marching to the beat of your own drum, charting your own path forward.

Because entrepreneurs are unique, your lifestyle is, too. The entrepreneur's life is unconventional and represents ultimate freedom. You are free to work from wherever you choose, whenever you choose. You can work at midnight from an airplane or from your kitchen table at noon. You can hold meetings with clients halfway around the world through videoconferencing that costs nothing, or meet with them at their neighborhood Starbucks.

The world is truly your oyster, and all you have to do is collect the pearls.

Sounds like total freedom, right?

If you are or have ever been an entrepreneur, you are probably reading through these descriptions and saying, "Yeah, right." Because while many of these traits reflect the life of the entrepreneur, this is not the complete picture.

Here's the stone cold truth: being an entrepreneur is hard, probably the hardest thing someone can do. The idea of freedom is alluring, and that freedom always exists—in theory. While you might not have a dragon boss breathing down your back, what threatens your freedom is the immense responsibility of running your own business.

Everything, from the biggest crises to the tiniest nuisance, suddenly becomes your problem. Moreover, you—and you alone—are responsible for making sure money comes into the business, and it does so on time. You don't have to punch in or punch out of a time clock. Why? Because now that you're an entrepreneur, you feel the pressure to work twenty-four/seven. Congratulations!

We haven't even gotten to stress levels. Suffice it to say, being stressed out will now become the baseline for your life. Toby Thomas, CEO of EnSite Solutions (they're number 188 on the Inc. 500), likes to use the analogy of a man riding a lion. "People look at him and think, 'This guy's really got it together! He's brave!' And the man riding the lion is thinking, 'How the hell did I get on a lion, and how do I keep from getting eaten?' "[1]

But then there are the rewards. Those of us who stick it out and see it through until we succeed do so because we have an abiding passion for our work. We live to be creative and to contribute meaningfully to the world, through our special gifts and unique visions. We know that life is short, and we want ours to count. We want to live life on our terms. We want to be fulfilled.

If this sounds like you, then you're going to want to read on.

My love affair for the entrepreneurial spirit is nearly two decades old. I've worked and collaborated with countless

---

1   Bruder, Jessica. "The Psychological Price of Entrepreneurship," INC. Magazine, September 2013. http://www.inc.com/magazine/201309/jessica-bruder/psychological-price-of-entrepreneurship.html

entrepreneurs since the early 2000s, and I have deep respect and admiration for those brave souls who strike out on their own, blazing their own trails. I've been inspired to take a similar leap in my own life—and unfortunately, I've also fallen into some of the same traps. If you are exhausted, unhappy, overtaxed, and overworked, I can relate. The overwhelming majority of us suffer or have suffered from Lifestyle Deficit Disorder™—LDD. I believe LDD is the single greatest affliction plaguing entrepreneurs today.

Wouldn't you like to discover a way out from under the overwhelming number of hats you wear? Doesn't it sound appealing to create more time and energy in your life—and increase revenue at the same time?

I intimately understand the challenges entrepreneurs face. From time management, to work-life balance, to wealth cultivation, I know the struggles. I have been through them myself, having struck out on my own and created my own business. I left the creature comforts of big brokerage and the corporate office with no overhead or bills to hang out my own shingle, build a brand, rebuild a client base, and develop a marketing strategy.

Back when I still worked in big brokerage, I had two partners, a full staff, a steadily increasing income—and a raging case of LDD. Since stepping out on my own, I've merged one company, maintained an independent consulting and online investment management firm, founded two nonprofits, and run a real estate syndicate. I own a bar and restaurant, and I just began a goat-dairy operation on my farm. The term "serial entrepreneur" fits. The best part: my LDD is in remission.

I know how exhausting it can be, how run down you get as an entrepreneur, how so often you find yourself thinking, "I was supposed to have *more* freedom, not give up every spare second!" It wasn't always easy for me—I struggled to strike a healthy work-life balance with only one going concern. I was thirsty for a purpose, hungry to find a way to do the things that were most important to me instead of just trying to earn and save money. And then one day, after years of frustration, I woke up.

How I Woke Up

Here's the part where I tell you my own story, so you know this stuff isn't theoretical: I eat my own cooking.

It was a big step for me to leave safe and secure big brokerage and start my own investment firm. After years of working for others, I was finally operating independently, without conflicts, in a way that let me serve my clients better than before. In stepping out and going on my own, I endeavored to "right" all the wrongs I saw on Wall Street—commissions, being married to stocks and bonds (having no real estate avenue to offer), selling products that didn't make sense. Basically, I wanted to eliminate all of these conflicts of interest. I was fired up and passionate about what I was doing, unconstrained, and invigorated by the idea that I had the freedom to do as I wished during the workweek.

A month later, the market crashed.

In that environment, procuring new clients was hard. Investors and business owners alike were financially paralyzed—and rightfully so. My husband's business suffered as manufacturing and industrial engineering ground to a halt. For the next two years, all we were doing was work, work, work. It was a grind that only someone like you can understand, because you've probably been living that same "dream." My husband and I woke up one morning and said, it's time to hit the reset button. Have you ever felt the need to hit the reset button?

On top of a recession and a new business, our seven-year-old daughter was having trouble in first grade. She attended one of the best private schools in Charleston, South Carolina, a school I had vetted thoroughly. Five or six meetings with her teacher and headmaster later, the school was telling us that she needed to be medicated because they thought she had ADD. She could not copy the teacher's writing on the chalkboard quickly enough.

Know that my daughter's handwriting, then and now, is impeccable. She's a bit of a perfectionist (ahem, not sure where that came from!). If she messed up one letter of a word, she would erase that whole word and write it over again. As a result, sometimes she didn't finish what the teacher was writing on the board—and then she would have to miss P.E. I believe that breaking out of the classroom and running around a little bit is exactly what a seven-year-old needs. But no, she couldn't go to P.E. because first she had to finish writing what was on the board.

Several conferences in, the school mandated a doctor's evaluation for ADD. But the teachers and the school had it wrong—the doctor denied their suspicion of ADD.

It was time for my daughter and I to make a deal. If she copied down everything from the board in time, I would take her for gelato. This worked for a while. Then, after a long stretch of compliance with copying the board, one day she didn't. I picked her up from school that day and, upon discovering that she hadn't completed the board, I pulled over and asked her what the reason was. She looked me in the eye and said, "You know, Mom, it would be one thing if the teacher would just tell us what we had to write versus us copying everything from the board. Anybody can copy stuff from a board! But not everybody knows how to spell February! February is tricky, with that 'r' in it. I know how to spell it." It was the month of February and the information on the board always started with the day's date.

"So it's just not worth it to me to copy it from the board. But if the teacher would just call it out to us, maybe we would all learn how to spell and have to think about what we were writing."

"Let's go get some gelato," I said. I had tears in my eyes because my seven-year-old knew better than her school, her teacher, and *me*. Shame on us for putting her on the performance train by making her copy a chalkboard. She saw through that task for what it was—and she wanted something more. Something better.

I realized then that my seven-year-old daughter was calling out the teacher and offering her a better method, one I totally agreed with. Something shifted in me. Perhaps it was that I hadn't been present enough with the situation to be a better advocate for my daughter and defend her from day one against copying a chalkboard when her handwriting was perfect. I hadn't lobbied to let her have recess and gelato, whether she finished the busy work or not. Wasn't that the main takeaway? I hadn't taken the time to seek my daughter's perspective sooner—or to dial in to mine. I was too busy. My LDD had run rampant, and I was no longer focusing on the things that mattered.

That's when it hit me: *we're in the wrong school.* Not only that, but I wasn't present with my kids the way I wanted to be. Time to hit reset.

Now, keep in mind this was happening at the same time my husband and I were working around the clock, desperate to make a new business thrive and keep another one afloat. It was time we got back to our core values of family and meaningful connection and not simply letting our days and the people in our days dictate how those days would go.

Not long before all this was happening, we'd heard about a public school in the town of Silverton, Colorado (where we had recently bought a commercial property) that had just received close to $10 million in grants. It was a small school—just seventy children, grades K through 12. Silverton, with one paved road, nestled in the majestic San Juan Mountains of Southwest Colorado, was going to be the perfect reset button.

So we said, "That's it. We're going." Family first, with a dose of faith that my business would survive a move across the country! That was my new attitude.

We moved to Silverton to create a new experience for all of us. Life in Silverton is very much *Little House on the Prairie*: you can go a week without getting in your car. It's a fantastic environment for raising kids, indulging in the outdoors, and hitting that reset button. *Very* family first.

And that's how we lived for three-and-a-half years. We put our family first. Ironically, my business headquartered in SC was up 20 percent-plus every year we lived in Colorado.

I understand that not everyone can move from suburban Charleston to the hills of Colorado just to improve life for themselves and their children—and not everyone would want to. Believe me, there were plenty of challenges and complications. But if you constantly put out all the reasons why you cannot do things, you'll always find a reason why not to make a move—why you can't hit reset. Moving to Colorado was one of the best things we ever did for our children *and* ourselves.

Starting She CLIMBS

Since moving to Silverton, I've watched so many things in my life flourish, including my capacity for "giving back." In 2015, I started a nonprofit called She CLIMBS. Our mission is to build self-confidence and self-esteem in women and young girls by climbing mountains; namely, Mount Kilimanjaro. I've been climbing mountains for over a decade now and I've met many women in transition, whether in passing or via my financial planning practice. They are divorced, widowed, or empty-nesters, women who are suddenly wondering, who the heck am I? What am I doing with my life? And I cannot tell you how many women who would never have dreamt of putting on hiking boots and going rugged have said to me, "I don't know what it is, but the next time you go on a mountain, take me with you. I want to climb a mountain."

She CLIMBS embodies everything that matters to me: service, nature, transformation, and helping people go for it. You don't want to climb a mountain? Run a marathon. Start a nonprofit. The main thing is, do something. Don't just sit there answering your email and letting LDD take a firmer grasp. Hire somebody else to manage your email. Get out and live.

Why did I start She CLIMBS? When I got married, and we started to think about children, I prayed for boys. And God gave me two girls. That's the "She" part.

I've always loved climbing because you've got no cell phones, no connection to the outside world. It's the best reset button ever, a way to steady yourself in mind, body, and spirit. That's the "CLIMBS" part: the Center for Leadership In Mind, Body, and Spirit. Since 2003, summiting a mountain has been my ultimate Perfect Day.

Before 2003, I hadn't put a lot of time or thought into what a "perfect day" would be for me. Frankly, I hadn't put *any* time or thought into it. I was fettered by my LDD, exhausted and frustrated; I was chasing the almighty dollar against the strain of being a woman in a man's world. Not too many years later, with young children, all my family got were the leftovers. I didn't even know how desperately I needed to hit the reset button. But when my life coach had me write out my Perfect Day, I laid the first brick on the path that would lead me to where I am today: helping clients create their Perfect Day Lifestyle around a simple, attainable vision of what makes them happy, fulfilled, and free.

<u>My</u> <u>Perfect</u> <u>Day</u>

Date 2003

Captain announcing
on NYC arrival
at 2 pm - 17/
more hours!

I am so at rest that I
didn't even make it through
take-off my going home. I reflect &
I am so filled with the news and disbelief—
I did it — God carried me the
whole way, but I did it. Dollar
Signs—! that is all I can
think of right Now besides looking out
the window when we land & seeing
Tony & "the boys". The hoops Tony
had to go through to get ATC
to allow them on this runway! I
wonder how much endorsements
will come IN & with who?
what are the headlines going to
say? Not a moment later the
Stewardess brings me a paper &
a bloody Mary — Youngest American
Female Climbs Seven Summits.
Couldn't they come up with something
a little snazzier than that?
Crazy Charlestonian Climbs
14m all would've been a little
better! I've worked so hard for
this headline but can't wait even
more for the next —
Climber donates 100% of endorsements
to She CLIMBS — a national
school & center for female teens &
young adults that battles self esteem
and Confidence. I dare to think it'll come in

I'm living proof that this doesn't always happen overnight. She CLIMBS was a part of my Perfect Day vision in 2003, but it took twelve years for it to become a reality. I finally achieved the She CLIMBS piece of my Perfect Day in 2015 when my eldest daughter, my climbing partner Suzanne, and her daughter summited with me on the first She CLIMBS adventure. It was worth the wait. When you plant that seed, and then do the work to nourish and cultivate it, your magical Perfect Days can go from dream to reality. But first you have to plant the seed.

She CLIMBS summited Kilimanjaro just weeks before I started writing this book. This expedition included my husband and ten-year-old daughter, who became my second daughter to summit. It was an extraordinary day for all of us. We summited with another ten-year-old, an eleven-year-old, and a fifty-year-old woman and her husband. There may have been a forty-year age difference between some of the climbers, but I can promise you, the experience was life-changing for all of them.

That's what I want this book to be for you. I want it to change your life. I want it to take you wherever you want to go, whether that means the peak of Kilimanjaro or sailing a distant sea, giving a TED talk in front of hundreds of people, or launching your fifth startup. This book is meant to be a guidebook to help you launch yourself into the life you've always dreamed of. Not anyone else's—the life *you* want. The life you deserve to live.

The lessons I've learned over the years—whether from client experiences, in boardrooms, collaborating with uber-successful business owners, or on a mountaintop—have shaped me into a better, more balanced business owner and individual. This has allowed me to lead a very rich life, growing wealth in both the financial and non-financial aspects of my life. Moreover, I have had the privilege of working with many brilliant, ambitious entrepreneurs, coaching them in business, finance, and lifestyle. I have learned from my associates and clients that it is possible to have a Perfect Day. In fact, it's possible to have a lot of them.

This book is chock full of gems of wisdom mined from decades of working as a financial advisor and business consultant, and from the entrepreneurial allegiances I have formed over the years. It is supplemented with what I've learned from my own trials and errors as I endeavored to find the right work-life balance to become a successful entrepreneur and a fulfilled human being. For too long, I thought a Perfect Day was a mythical creature—or a horizon I could never reach.

Perhaps you feel the same. So many people are counting on you. You've got big dreams and big plans, and there simply aren't enough hours in the day to achieve them. Maybe you dream about taking time off "someday"—but only once you've earned it. Right now, you can't imagine when that someday will be. How can you possibly enjoy a Perfect Day with everything you have to do and accomplish?

The Perfect Day is less about perfection and more about clarity and freedom. It means crafting the lifestyle you truly want, not the life you're inadvertently leading because you didn't think you had any other choice. As you define it further in the following pages, your Perfect Day may surprise you. For many of my clients, it's quite different from the picture they've had in their heads all their lives: shiny baubles and a huge bank account. A tent on Kilimanjaro with my ten-year-old is a far cry from visions of cars and boats and planes. Those may be fantastic shiny baubles, yes—but for me, they are full of empty promise, glimmering mirages lacking true depth.

The fast pace of today's business world, made all the faster by advances in technology and travel, along with the cutthroat, competitive atmosphere in which we all are cast, has skewed our perspective of reality. We are always on the go, always feeling that pressure to do more, earn more, take on more. It's like we are all racing on this hamster wheel—and we haven't even realized we have the choice to step off.

You're leading this life because you want to pursue excellence and make some money in the process. You were brave enough to answer the call of the entrepreneur because you wanted freedom. But somewhere along the way, you took a wrong step. Your ambitions derailed you. You wanted freedom, but you settled for worry, exhaustion, and stress. You slipped off the mountain path and now you're hanging on for dear life.

So how do you get back on track? How do you recover your strength to summit the mountain? How do you create your Perfect Day? And then, how do you turn that day into your Perfect Week, Month, Year, *Life*?

How to Use This Book

In the chapters that follow, you're going to fast track to envisioning and implementing your Perfect Day. You may not yet know why you need a Perfect Day, but soon you will see: it's not only the antidote for LDD, but a recipe for a thriving business. You can live a life filled with Perfect Days *now*. You don't have to wait until you retire. You don't have to get out of the business in order to experience the life you want. In fact, a Perfect Day Lifestyle will encourage your business toward efficiencies, increase capability, and enhance all aspects of communication.

Think of this book as a kind of Sherpa to help you summit your own personal and professional mountain. The heavy lifting is here in these pages, but you have to put one foot in front of the next and keep climbing.

Not sure if you have LDD? In Chapters 1-2, we'll talk more about Lifestyle Deficit Disorder and how to diagnose yourself. If you're besieged by a lack of time and energy—and if you have trouble delegating tasks—chances are you have LDD. And as anyone who has struggled with an addiction knows, the first step to getting help is to admit you have a problem.

This is especially hard for entrepreneurs to hear, much less internalize. You are used to doing everything on your own! You have no problem making sacrifices for your success. But that's why it is all the more important for you to recognize you may have a problem—that something in your life may be amiss.

In Chapter 3, let's commit to taking a closer look at the Perfect Day. Remember, the Perfect Day does not mean perfection; it means freedom. How do you develop a Perfect Day Lifestyle? This is the area in which most of us experience a deficit, so the reasonable next step is to understand what your life might look like if you *didn't* have that deficit. In other words, what have you been missing out on? We've identified your problem: now what's the solution?

Once we get to Chapters 4 and 5, you'll get some hands-on opportunities to lay out a clear path from where you are now to the Perfect Day Lifestyle you envision. We'll talk about gratitude and why we need it; then we'll take an inventory of your assets and you'll complete the vision focuser. In Chapter 6, you'll drill down deeper into what your "wobble" is, and you'll have a chance to engage with your own personal affirmations to construct your Perfect Day.

Next you'll identify and hone the tools you need to implement your customized Perfect Day. In Chapter 7, you'll craft a Commander's Intent and learn how to integrate this powerful, transformative practice into your work, relationships, and life. In Chapter 8, you'll identify your genius and celebrate your "You-ness." In Chapter 9, you'll learn tips and strategies to better organize your time. In Chapter 10, you'll explore ways to increase your productivity, and in Chapter 11, you'll get a crash course in what is often a difficult area for entrepreneurs: delegating. Just as you must be strategic with your intentions and your time, so, too, must you be prudent with your efforts and energy, to make sure you allocate yourself enough space and joy to do the things that make you, you.

By this point, you will be well on your way to the Perfect Day, with a detailed, in-depth roadmap for how to get from A to B. You'll have envisioned a new kind of lifestyle, one that is balanced and fulfilling, a solid foundation on which to build success and prosperity. Now you're ready for the final touch.

Chapter 12 is devoted to the greatest asset you'll ever have: relationships. I believe the most important aspects of wealth creation are vulnerability, authenticity, and that personal touch. So in Chapter 13, we'll look at how cultivating a strong relationship with the right financial planner can help you stay true to your heart's desires as you live out your Perfect Day Lifestyle.

With a little bit of creative and intentional strategizing, you can make room for all of the things that are important to you: family, finances, health, recreation, and, yes, business (and maybe a few shiny baubles, too). You can live out your Perfect Day, *every* day.

Let's DO IT!

||||||||||||||||||||||||||||

PART ONE
The Problem:
Lifestyle Deficit Disorder

||||||||||||||||||||||||||||

Your work is going to fill a large part of
your life, and the only way to be truly
satisfied is to do what you believe is great
work. And the only way to do great work
is to love what you do. If you haven't
found it yet, keep looking. Don't settle.
As with all matters of the heart, you'll
know when you find it. And, like any
great relationship, it just gets better and
better as the years roll on. So keep looking
until you find it. Don't settle.

–STEVE JOBS

CHAPTER 1

What is Lifestyle Deficit Disorder, And Do You Have It?

||||||||||||||||||||||||||||||||

"It's the possibility of having a dream come true that makes life interesting."
–PAULO COELHO, THE ALCHEMIST

Sandy and Fred are clients of mine. When they first came to see me, the "problem" at hand was to fix a cash flow and retirement planning conundrum. They expected a strictly financial discussion of liquidity and financial assets; instead, I had them engage in the Perfect Day Pyramid process, which ultimately led them to write out their Perfect Day. A bit perplexed, Sandy and Fred played along. In the end, they imagined themselves surrounded by their children and grandchildren in a vacation rental, a beautiful ski-in-ski-out home in the Colorado Rockies. It was their dream trip. *That* was their Perfect Day.

They never took the trip. Instead, years later, I was sitting with Sandy in the waiting area outside a hospital emergency room. Fred was on the operating table, undergoing emergency surgery after having suffered a heart attack.

All I could think was: Sandy, here we are in the ER. Your husband might die. Why didn't you take that vacation?

Symptom #1: Not Enough Time

Like many professionals and business owners, Sandy and Fred rarely took vacations. How could they? They would contend that getting away, even for a couple of days, was quite difficult. Right? Being out of reach—contemplating the number of emails and voicemails that would no doubt accumulate—makes taking time off utterly unappealing.

Most people I work with are passionate about their businesses, passionate about being industry leaders, and passionate about creating the next great product or service. Unfortunately, all too often, their passion for the business takes over and they become all but enslaved to their businesses. There's never enough time. Every minute goes toward building their business, instead of crafting their lives ... *and then* building a business that fits *around* their life.

The question is, how? And what will you do with all that time?

Symptom #2: Inability to Delegate

If you're anything like me, delegating does not come naturally. The whole reason you got into business in the first place was because it stoked a fire inside you—it lit you up, turned on your brain, and made you come alive. And if you're like most entrepreneurs, the business was or is *you*—at least in the early days. Your company wouldn't have survived without your blood, sweat, and tears. No wonder it's so hard to step away.

You don't have to be a control freak to have a hard time delegating tasks. But unless you learn to delegate, your business will always run you instead of you running your business. If you want freedom, delegation is the name of the game.

Symptom #3: Worries Over Money

You wouldn't believe how many people I work with who, although they're making great money, are consumed by fear of losing money. That's the number one issue I hear, time and again. Once we scrape past the ego-driven "everything's fine" nonsense, we inevitably end up in conversations about fear of not having enough: not having enough money to fund a lifestyle now, and not having enough to fund college, retirement, travel, healthcare, or whatever may happen down the road.

All these people can think about is paying the bills. Here's a further irony—most of the time, they don't even have a good system in place for doing so. Most of the people I work with bring in plenty of money, but they lack efficient systems regarding cash flow, bills, collecting, and other financial matters. They don't like the idea of paying somebody to do their books, which is counterintuitive, because if they could offload some of those mundane tasks, they could be more productive in their businesses.

Or they could get a life.

The Diagnosis

Not enough time, inability to delegate, worries over money: these are the primary symptoms of Lifestyle Deficit Disorder. People suffering from LDD are sick—and most of the time, they don't even know they're sick. They've constructed their whole lives around their businesses. Work comes first, and their hobbies, passions, projects, friends, and family members get what's left over. Their whole life amounts to a big pile of leftovers. Everything—and everyone—else suffers.

What's included in the "everything else?" Their marriages. Their sex lives. Their health and fitness. Their relationships with their children. Community activities? You've got to be kidding. These people barely have time to breathe. If they aren't sleeping with their cell phones by their beds, they aren't sleeping.

When I tell clients to "get a life," I don't mean simply creating a business and a financial life that works. Of course you want to generate the money you need to survive, and then some. What I want is for my clients to find that elusive holy grail that practically every sentient business owner, professional, solopreneur, and entrepreneur wants to find but secretly doubt its very existence: **a healthy, balanced lifestyle with a thriving business that makes you want to get out of bed each morning.** A lifestyle in which the Perfect Day becomes not only attainable, but a frequent occurrence.

Is balance even possible? Some people bristle at the first mention of "balance." They think it sounds hippy-dippy or unattainable. They're afraid it means losing out on something or having to make sacrifices they aren't willing to make. Most people, driven by fear, put every possible moment into their business. Whatever is left over—including, time, money, and energy—is rationed for themselves and their loved ones.

But they will be the first to tell you that there's simply never enough of any of those things. For the entrepreneur who's suffering from LDD, time, money, and energy are always in short supply.

Eliminate that Muffin Top

I'll tell you what I think about a lot: the muffin top. You know the muffin top—it's that middle-aged spread that people get when they eat too much, drink too much, and exercise and rest too little. The muffin top, which afflicts both genders equally, symbolizes the lack of self-love and self-care that accompany Lifestyle Deficit Disorder.

Look down—how comfy are you with yours? Our muffin tops do more than make us look and feel unattractive to ourselves and our sex partners. For those of us who are parents and grandparents, being out of shape sets a terrible example for our kids. Too often, young people are staring down a crisis of childhood obesity because, like us, they eat badly, don't exercise, and spend their whole lives staring at their devices.

The problem with carrying extra fat around the middle is that it hastens heart disease, stroke, and—according to the latest research—even Alzheimer's and other forms of memory disorder. We are literally killing ourselves, one muffin at a time.

But sometimes it takes a trip to the ER, as it did in the case of Fred and Sandy, to make us realize just how great a risk we're running by putting our businesses first and our lives second. Will you wait to create your Perfect Day until after your ER moment?

People know how to take good care of themselves. Everybody knows the secret of losing weight—eat well and move more. Just about all the business owners I know and work with have gym memberships, but they often haven't seen the inside of a gym for months, or even years. They need caffeine to get going in the morning and Ambien to bring them down at night, because they can't shut off and detach at the end of the day. If you talk to them, they seem low-energy and frustrated. They are operating in the past or the future, but never the present.

Curing LDD: Moving Closer to Your Perfect Day

Moving to Silverton was a big part of how we cured our Lifestyle Deficit Disorder. The big move was a metaphor to live by: we honored a rather kind and gentle "ER moment" (others aren't so lucky) to heed the call of our Perfect Day. We chose doing what was best for our children and our family—at the risk of our businesses.

True, physically moving across the country helped me get away from some of the everyday pitfalls that were holding me back. But it doesn't always require such a drastic change. The move shifted my perspective and changed the pace of my life. And ever since, because I was able to make this move and embrace these changes, I've been able to help other entrepreneurs reclaim their own lives, experientially and financially, from a place of authenticity and personal experience.

I'll be honest: it wasn't easy. It took a lot of soul-searching and careful planning for us to successfully reset our lives. We had to first understand what our values and priorities were and then design our lives so that they reflected those values. In particular, we had to start making big changes in how we managed our time and energy, and we had to learn how to effectively delegate.

If this resonates with you, it might be time for a self-diagnosis. Do you have LDD? If so, how is it affecting your life? I don't just mean your work life—I mean your life in every moment you live it. How often does your business intrude on your free time? Are you sacrificing your lifestyle because you're worried you won't make enough money? Do you find yourself tired and lacking energy? Are you frustrated that you're spending so much time on your business that you don't have enough time left to spend with your family and friends?

What "reset button" do you pine for? There's one inside of all of us.

What ER moment is lurking around the corner that you can sidestep, today?

I want to catch you now, *before* the Emergency Room. Before the divorce. Before the muffin top. Before you spend untold discretionary dollars on your Ambien prescription. I want to show you the small shifts you can make so that you can have a life again—instead of just a lifetime of work.

Fred and Sandy's story has a happy ending. In the hospital waiting room that day, Sandy looked me squarely in the eyes and said, "We're going to take that trip to Colorado."

Fred recovered, and they did go to Colorado. They've taken many vacation trips in the years since.

If you have Lifestyle Deficit Disorder, keep reading. As a recovered LDD-er myself—and as someone who's helped others cure their LDD—I can relate to what you're going through. I can also offer hope. There *is* a way out of the slump you're in, and I've charted that journey in this book.

First, let's talk about your happy meter. Is it broken?

CHAPTER 2

Fixing Your Broken Happy Meter

||||||||||||||||||||||||||||||

Happiness is not a goal ...
it's a by-product of a life well lived.
–ELEANOR ROOSEVELT

I'm going to go out on a limb here and assume you aren't happy. You may be happy in some ways, sure. But if you were 100 percent happy, you'd be living your Perfect Day every day—and you wouldn't need this book.

When my clients say, "I'm not happy," I tell them: "The problem is, your happy meter may be broken. You've got a broken yardstick for measuring happiness." The question is not, are you happier than your neighbor? The question is this: Have you fallen out of the habit of dreaming how great your life could be and then making those dreams come true?

Entrepreneurially minded individuals typically set the happiness bar at an extremely high level. They watch Tony Robbins videos and believe they can have it all. So they work like crazy to make the money to fund what they think will be a fabulous life. But there's no balance. They end up with overwork and misery. Reactivity. The nefarious muffin top.

These folks are great at setting goals for their businesses, but have they ever set—and kept—meaningful goals in their personal lives? Do they start their business planning for the year by calculating just how much time they will spend with their spouses and children?

Do they say: "This year, I will make the time to nourish myself properly, physically and spiritually?" Do they set goals like: "This year, I'm going to climb Mount Kilimanjaro, run a marathon, or do something else that drags me away from my desk. I'm going to turn off my cell phone and experience life instead of letting life run over me?"

Most of the time, they don't. The voice in their head convinces them that, if they do switch and start focusing on lifestyle, they'll lose money or their business will suffer. They never ask, "What happens if I spend too much time on my business? How will that be detrimental to my personal life— to my weight, my health, my relationships?"

What if you adopted a you-centric way of living instead of the business-centric approach that may have grossed you a solid income ... but has netted you a meager life?

Don't Confuse the Means for the Ends

Everyone is working for money. But ask yourself this: What's the money for?

Tony Robbins teaches that there's a difference between "means goals" and "end goals." Most people confuse the end for the means. They say, "I want to be a millionaire," and they think that being a millionaire is the end goal. In reality, it's just a means to what they really want, which is a feeling.

What's the feeling?

The feeling that they're successful.

The irony is that they could have that feeling right now if they just took a look at their lives and saw how much they have already accomplished. Otherwise, they're going to throw away all the time they could have been fly-fishing or climbing Kilimanjaro. They'll just be returning emails and setting new client meetings while life literally passes them by.

Do you need money to survive in life? Of course you do. I'm a financial advisor, for goodness sake! I'm the last one to denigrate the importance of money in life.

What I am saying is that when your stress is on money, you're going to end up with way too much stress ... and not enough money.

Most of us don't plan on saying, "I wish I'd spent more time working" when we're on our deathbeds. So why are we saying it now? In *The Road to Character*, David Brooks makes a distinction between what he calls résumé virtues and epitaph virtues. Your résumé virtues have to do with your titles, your credentials, and your income. Your epitaph virtues have to do with the love you shared with the people around you, the service you provided to your community, and the contributions you made. As the expression goes, "What you take with you is what you leave behind."

I'm asking you to lift your head up from your laptop, from your cell phone, from your tablet, and ponder the epitaph virtues you'd like to be remembered for. In other words, we want to start with the end of our lives in mind, so that we can make our lives today that much better. We must start every day and end every day with those epitaph virtues as the focus. It's about setting goals, not just for the business, but for our personal lives—and then putting the energies and intentionality around those personal goals so they come true.

I'm telling you, if you do that, the money will flow in ways that are all but unimaginable now.

Sir Richard Branson—whom I consider the world's most successful entrepreneur, not simply as a function of his wealth and accomplishments, but by how much he gives back to the Earth—invented what I think is the best happy meter of all. Branson wrote a letter entitled "Dear Stranger, Letters on the Subject of Happiness," which he keeps on his website, www.virgin.com/richard-branson/my-tips-for-happiness. Below is one of my favorite quotes from the letter.

I know I'm fortunate to live an extraordinary life, and that most people would assume my business success, and the wealth that comes with it, have brought me happiness. But they haven't; in fact it's the reverse. I am successful, wealthy, and connected because I am happy.

–Sir Richard Branson

A Holistic Approach to Gains and Losses

There's a fascinating story about lottery winners and people who have lost limbs. When people win the lottery, initially, they are exultant. They've got all the money in the world! But then things start to change. The initial happiness fades. They start getting calls from distant relatives they've never met who say they need $15,000 for Cousin June to finally get that operation. The lottery winners feel bad when they have to say no, but they're getting dozens of similar requests.

When they go to the grocery store, the grocer looks at them differently. No more free samples—you're a millionaire!

If they don't blow through all the money in a year or two—which is unfortunately all too common—they often have to move to a new community where no one knows them as lottery winners. Overall, surveys indicate that the happiness of lottery winners is actually lower than it was before they bought the winning tickets.

Contrast their experience with that of people who lose limbs in accidents. Initially, as would be expected, these individuals go through periods of profound depression. But after a while, if they get therapy, they often reach a point where they're grateful for the rest of their limbs and the physical abilities they had always taken for granted. In a supreme twist of irony, people who lose limbs statistically are happier than lottery winners a year or two after those incidents.

To put a bow on this: a group of veterans, all of whom had lost limbs in Iraq or Afghanistan, climbed Kilimanjaro side by side with us on our last climb. They were as happy as anyone

I've ever seen. It reminded me that busy entrepreneurs often *think* they know what will make them happy—more time, more money, a more efficient staff. But what they really need is to dive deep into their core values to understand that the happiness "problem" they've identified is, in fact, not the problem.

They've been running toward an empty goal, a broken happy meter that ensures happiness is always just beyond the horizon. And of course, when happiness is forever moving a few miles ahead of where you are, you'll never quite get there.

Play the Values Game

If money were no object, where would you like to be in a year? What would you be doing? Who would be there with you?

Chances are, whatever you want to do—within reason—is attainable within the next twelve months. It's not about finding the money. It's about finding the commitment. Hard-driven entrepreneurs who see life almost entirely in financial terms believe that you can solve pretty much any problem by throwing money at it.

It turns out, that's not true.

If you think you're throwing a lot of money at your spouse now, just wait and see how much money you're throwing when the divorce decree becomes final. If you think you're spending a lot of money on your kids, compensating them out of guilt for the lack of time and attention you're able to give them, wait until you get the therapy bill a few years down the line. It's like the old Midas muffler ad: you can pay now, or you can pay later.

But you've got another choice. Figure out what you really want. Budget the time. Then, and only then, figure out how you'll pay for it. People who come back from Kilimanjaro, or fly-fishing, or marathons, or a vacation working for Habitat for Humanity, return to their business lives energized, focused, and above all, happy.

And if you don't think the goddess of money likes happy people, then you just don't know that goddess.

Jon LoDuca of The Wisdom Link, a consultant of mine for years, helped lead me to the concept of a life-driven business. Jon coaches, speaks, and writes about the issues and opportunities of today's entrepreneurs. For the last fifteen years, he's helped hundreds of his clients build life-centered businesses. Given this, I took the opportunity to ask him about his take on Lifestyle Deficit Disorder. He sees the root of Lifestyle Deficit Disorder as "a systemic issue business owners encounter from the very beginning." He recognized that, if the business is put first, the lifestyle will always come last.

"Traditionally," Jon says, "business owners have started out with a Business Model based on an established industry. The entrepreneur pours their time and energy into the business. The Business Model then deducts what it needs and leaves whatever is left over for the owner to take home. That margin of time and energy dictates the owner's Life Model—and that of his/her family.

"The problem with this is that while there is an unlimited amount of money out there, there is not an unlimited amount of time or energy in the life of the entrepreneur.

"By starting with a desired Life Model, a business owner can identify priorities and live by them, defining creative constraints that support his/her vision. All decisions, business and otherwise, can then be tested against the Life Model vision."

The Wisdom Link created the graphic below to illustrate the difference between a Business-Centered Life model and a Life-Centered Business model. Which one describes the life *you're* living right now?

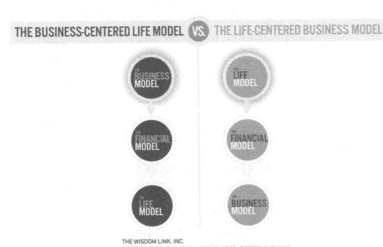

THE WISDOM LINK, INC.

TM 2017, The Wisdom Link, Inc. All rights reserved. No part of this material may be reproduced in any form, or by any means whatsoever, without written consent from the publisher.

The Prescription for the Perfect Day

I believe that, if you want to live life to the fullest, you must first put your energy, your time, and your money into your own life. Meet the needs of yourself and your loved ones first. Then allow your business to grow around those vital priorities—instead of dominating your life, as it does for most people.

Either you mold the business around your lifestyle, or your lifestyle becomes sublimated to the eternal quest to return the next email. If business always comes first, your life becomes ... well, leftovers.

The irony is that we are so stunningly loyal to our businesses, but our businesses are seldom as loyal to us. Employees don't take the mission as seriously as we do. Clients we serve will leave. Here we are, giving the best years of our lives and the best moments of all the days of our lives to something that doesn't love us back.

Meanwhile, we are surrounded by people who *would* love us back—our spouses, our children, our friends, our families—if only we had time and energy to show them the love we feel.

We are proactive about work and reactive about everything else. When you see it put that starkly, doesn't it become abundantly clear that such an approach makes no sense? There's the old expression: We trade our health to gain wealth, and then we need to use our wealth to regain our health. When we put work first, we put ourselves, our health, our nutrition, our exercise, our nurturing, and our relationships in a tie for last place. Leftovers. I don't know about you, but at our house at mealtime, no one ever gets very excited about leftovers.

We're always on, always connected to email, texts, voicemail, whatever. We are tethered to our technology. Imagine how much better our lives would be if we were just as connected to our spouses, our children, or even ourselves!

When I mention this to clients, I can see the look of panic in their eyes. Their belief is that if they put themselves and their needs and the needs of their loved ones first, they'll turn off the money spigot. Ironically, it works exactly the opposite. *When you do build in time for yourself first, you make even more money.* I know that sounds incredible, but that's been my experience and the experience of the people I counsel.

I'm not a therapist or a marriage counselor by any stretch. But people do say I'm the only financial services professional who throws money at her clients! I tell them to spend the money and take that vacation. Spend the money and buy that vacation house. Buy the boat. Buy the car they've dreamed of. I respect money: how it's made, how it's kept, how it grows, and what it is for. I honor the concept of lifestyle first. When you put your own lifestyle first and not your precious business, you recognize you cannot take it with you. What good is lying on your deathbed and having millions in the bank?

You know the story—a guy worth $20 million dies. Somebody who didn't know exactly how much money he had, asks, "How much did he leave behind?"

The answer: "All of it."

I can't describe what your Perfect Day entails—but *you* can. What I can do is give you a roadmap to help get you there.

Maybe you're an entrepreneur with a thriving business. Maybe you're saying, "Sure, I work too much, but I'm getting great results." The only problem—and it's a serious problem—is that your work life is all-consuming. I know, because I used to be a workaholic myself.

Stop asking why not. Stop asking how to make it happen. All too many entrepreneurs feel more like caged animals than like successful, free people. Putting your business first doesn't work.

I'm going to show you a better way. Now that we've diagnosed your LDD, we can talk about getting you on the right regimen to combat it—and how to live out your Perfect Day (nearly!) every day of your life.

||||||||||||||||||||||||||||||

PART TWO
The Solution: The Perfect Day

||||||||||||||||||||||||||||

When I was seventeen, I read a quote that went something like: "If you live each day as if it was your last, someday you'll most certainly be right." It made an impression on me, and since then, for the past thirty-three years, I have looked in the mirror every morning and asked myself: "If today were the last day of my life, would I want to do what I am about to do today?" And whenever the answer has been "no" for too many days in a row,

I know I need to change something.

–STEVE JOBS

CHAPTER 3
The Perfect Day Blueprint

||||||||||||||||||||||||||||||

Do what you can, with what you have, where you are.
—THEODORE ROOSEVELT

I t was a cold winter day in 2003 when I attended my first annual planning retreat led by my life coach, Claire Stuhr. I sat in a room with dozens of other stellar entrepreneurs— and I had absolutely no idea what I was in for.

Stacked in front of us were hundreds of magazines. Following instructions, I reached for the nearest pair of scissors and began to cut out pictures that inspired me, colors, sayings—you name it, if it inspired me, I cut it out. To this day, when I look at the collage I made that day, it brings an instant smile to my face. That collage is joy. Freedom.

Adventure. Love. It's all the things that, at that point in my life, came second, third, fourth, and fifth in my life—and that was on a lucky day.

I had a wicked case of LDD. Claire encouraged us to dream big, to reach for the things that most inspired us, the true desires of our hearts. When I made my collage, I cut out pictures from nature: tall green trees and majestic, snow-capped mountains. The air was crisp and clear, sunny but not too hot. A woman in climbing gear was descending the mountain, looking rejuvenated and content.

In my mind, that was me, coming down from Denali. My husband and children (not yet born) would be meeting me at the bottom with huge hugs.

Claire departed this earth when she lost her fight with breast cancer on June 1, 2006. But she left her mark on the hundreds of entrepreneurs she worked with, changing their lives for the better. Rarely a week goes by that I don't smile when I think of her, or rely on her entrepreneurial life wisdom. Over a decade later, the foundation of her legacy in *all* our lives is firmly rooted, and I believe that is in large part due to the Perfect Day exercise she trained us to complete annually.

Claire's process is different from the one I would come to develop, but I think of that day as my first foray in the Perfect Day sandbox. I was still a long way from coming up with my

Perfect Day methodology. To be honest, I was still a long way from living my Perfect Day. But the day I wrote about became a part of my new heartbeat, and that heartbeat meant tuning into a Perfect Day exercise annually, even if just for a day.

Once you recognize your Perfect Day, it will transform not only your day, but your year and your life. Even if you never look at it again, it becomes a part of you.

What *Is* a Perfect Day?

Have you ever had a Perfect Day? I'm not talking about one where all the lights turn green for you, your clothes are perfectly ironed and creased, your hair is exhibiting the perfect ratio of body and shine, and your mother-in-law calls just to pay you compliments.

I'm talking about a day where you shine; where you do the things that you love and are good at; where you spend time with the people who are most important to you, doing highly fulfilling activities that give you deep joy; a day where, at the end of it, you are able to rest easy, knowing your time was well spent.

That, to me, is the kind of Perfect Day that I strive for, not just for myself, but for my clients—and for you. The Perfect Day has nothing to do with perfection; it's all about living purposefully and meaningfully. It's about freedom.

My ultimate goal is to get entrepreneurs to a place where every single day is a version of their Perfect Day. That might sound overwhelming or downright impossible, but I can assure you that creating a Perfect Day blueprint is easier than you think.

Be Like the Maasai

You know who I'd want to be more like? The Maasai people of Africa.

Having spent a fair amount of time in Africa, I've come to admire the Maasai of Tanzania and Kenya. It's been said that if you put a Maasai tribesman in jail, and tell him he's got a thirty-day sentence to serve, he'll be dead practically overnight. They just don't understand the concept of thirty days from now; they only see where they are right now. They're present in the moment and choose not to see next month, but to focus on what they need today, now.

But what about us? We might be able to do a thirty-day jail sentence better than the Maasai, but what we've really created for ourselves is a life sentence, where work comes first and everything else is tied for last. As we've established, we don't even have a good yardstick for measuring our own happiness. We might say something like, "At least my life is better than my parents, or my neighbor, or so-and-so. So I'm happy." Since when has our personal happiness had anything to do with anyone else?

The Maasai don't compare themselves to one another. They're not jealous of other people's happiness: they're too busy looking at their own lives, in this present moment. I'm always amazed how, before we begin our expeditions, it's the women from the United States who are glued to their cell phones, trying to catch a Wi-Fi signal or see what they're missing back home. The Maasai who accompany us look peaceful and content, no phones in hand. Coincidence? I don't think so!

Know the 'Why' Before You Get to the 'How'

Why do we work? Is it to have *less* time to do all the things we don't call work?

No!

You work to fund your fun.

What are you going to do for fun this quarter? What are you going to do for fun next quarter? Why is this year going to be the best and most balanced year of your life? Those are the questions we should be asking—and yet we so rarely do.

It's not just about socking away a ton of money. It's about striking a balance between meeting your own needs and giving back, leaving this planet a better place than when you entered it, and contributing to the lives of others. It's about contributing to the spiritual growth of your children so that your kids become awesome participants in life as well. It's not just about the money.

I'm encouraging you to measure your life not just in terms of your net worth but your *net worthiness* as well. Are you growing through your experiences? Are you traveling and seeing new things? Are you learning? Are you increasing your capabilities? These are the qualities of the balanced entrepreneur.

As Morgan Freeman's character said in *Shawshank Redemption,* you either get busy living or you get busy dying. Which is it going to be?

Thinking through these things now, and actually living them, is a whole heck of a lot better than reaching sixty-five, retiring with a boatload of money, and saying, "I've always wanted to fly-fish, but I've got nobody to fly-fish with. I have no friends and my children are estranged."

I hear that so often. "For God's sake," I tell these people, "if you want to fly-fish, fly-fish today! Fly-fish this weekend!"

For all their talk about fly-fishing, they don't even know where to start. They don't even know how to Google fly-fishing and find a place where they can go learn how. I mean, of course they can do a Google search. But will they? Probably not. They think they don't deserve it, or they think they don't have the time, or they're afraid to spend the money. So they just keep on doing what they're best at, which is going to work.

Putting Your Money Where Your Mouth Is

It's time to turn your life on its ear. Most people start the year with a business plan. That's great, but what about the plan for the rest of your life—which, you might be surprised to discover, actually *is* your real life?

||||||||||||||||||||||||||||||||||||||||||||||||||||||||||||||||||||||||||||||||||||||||||||||||||||||||||||||||||||||||

SUGGESTED EXERCISE
Forget a Business Plan: Make a LIFE Plan

This exercise has two parts. For part one, you'll need a piece of paper. For part two, you'll need a calendar. It can be one of the big wall calendars or a pocketbook version, or you can use a calendar on your computer or a web app.

For **part one,** I want you to answer the following questions about the coming year:

1. How much time do you want to spend with your loved ones, spouse, and/or kids?
2. How many vacation days would you like to take?

3. What activities would really push the fun meter off the chart?

4. What activities or hobbies would you like to try that you've never gotten around to doing before? (Fly-fishing, pottery making, etc.)

Now that you're armed with your answers to **part one,** go through and circle the activities that need to go on the calendar. It's time to mark those dates on your calendar *now.*

The goal of this exercise is to block out your life activities first, *before* you start blocking out time for your business. Only after you have allotted time for your fun can you say, "Okay, I've got to make some money this year to make all these fun things happen. How am I going to fit that business plan around my life plan?"

Fill in your days for fly-fishing right now, because if you don't, you're going to schedule meetings every single day of the year, and you won't have a moment to get away. Here's the thing about fly-fishing: you have to be present. You've got to be constantly aware of your wrist action as you cast. It's beautiful, because it looks effortless, and in some ways, it is. When you're standing in your waders in a mountain stream, you're both literally and spiritually "in the flow."

You might think it's indulgent to make a list of things you want to do—fly-fish, ride your motorcycle, or climb Kilimanjaro. But those things aren't going to happen unless you get them on the calendar first.

I have a client who has twin twelve-year-old boys, and they love to fish. So he took them to Oregon. He did his homework and found that Bend is one of the best places for fly-fishing in the United States. He did his homework online and found the right companies that provided guides, gear, waders, fishing tackle, bait, and so on.

The funny thing is, my client hates to fish. He would just sit there by the side of the river, watching his kids knee-deep in the river, and he would take pictures and read a book. It was perfect for him. Why did he do it? He told me that his grandfather had been killed in a mob hit. His grandfather was sixty and he was ten when it happened. He's had all kinds of therapy, but he still lives his life haunted by the fear of sudden loss. He figured, if he didn't take his sons fly-fishing now, maybe something would happen and he would never have the chance.

Maybe nothing quite that stark has happened in your life. But the question remains: even if you aren't motivated by an awareness of your own mortality, why the hell aren't you out there fly-fishing right now?

There's a philosopher named G. I. Gurdjieff who taught that people are basically asleep. We sleepwalk through life, and it's our job as human beings to slap each other awake. Consider this chapter your wake-up call.

A Journey of Enlightenment: Beyond Retirement Planning

People frequently come to me and ask, "Could you help me? I need a retirement plan." In today's marketplace, there is no shortage of information or advisors when it comes to your finances. It may seem as if most financial advisors are offering the same thing. If you aren't willing to go deep on what you really, really want—besides retiring at sixty-five— then yes, basically all advisors are offering the same thing: a broken, empty financial plan.

What I would tell someone who comes to me looking for a retirement plan is this: "If you want to engage, this is what a planning engagement looks like." Then I walk them through a Gratitude Exercise—more on that in Chapter 4— and a Vision Focuser, which we'll discuss in greater depth in Chapter 5. At that point, they start to get it. They might say, "Oh my gosh! I'm selfish. I haven't given anything back," or "Why am I not spending more quality time with my family?" This is when reality smacks them in the face and they realize,

"I have a muffin top and I have to take Ambien every night to go to bed. What am I doing with my life?"

This is what sets my approach apart from other financial planners. It's not that complicated to figure out if someone will have enough money to retire. It's simple arithmetic. Anyone can do that. But that's not what people are looking for.

When someone says to me, "I need a retirement plan," I start thinking about what it is they *really* need.

I want my clients to recognize their Lifestyle Deficit Disorder and take steps to eradicate it. (Not many advisors assist their clients in this way.) When someone comes through my doors and says, "I want to plan for retirement," my desire is that they leave my office with more than just an understanding of the state of their finances. I want to give them something better. I want to give them their life back. I want to give them a lifetime of Perfect Days.

Launching the Perfect Day Process

Before we talk about how to implement your Perfect Day, I want to briefly talk about the three steps we must take to get there. These are crucial steps along the way—you can't skip over them, because they form the very foundation of the perspective shift that will take you from living with Lifestyle Deficit Disorder to living with freedom and purpose.

In Chapter 4, we'll look at Step One: Gratitude. I'll walk you through the same Gratitude Exercise I do with my clients to help them identify what truly matters to them. In Chapter 5 we'll cover Step Two, taking an Asset Inventory and completing a Vision Focuser, in which we focus in on your *true* assets and sort them accordingly. Chapter 6 is devoted to Step Three: Affirmations and Perfect Day Vision, where we tie it all up by affirming what your heart desires and putting those desires in action to create your Perfect Day.

Entrepreneurs of the world, unite! You have nothing to lose but your chains.

||||||||||||||||||||||||||||||

PART THREE
Three Steps on the Path: Gratitude, Asset Inventory and Vision Focuser, Affirmations and Perfect Day Vision

||||||||||||||||||||||||||||||

If you want happiness for an hour,

take a nap.

If you want happiness for a day,

go fishing.

If you want happiness for a year,

inherit a fortune.

If you want happiness for a lifetime,

help someone else.

–CHINESE PROVERB

CHAPTER 4

Step One:
Gratitude—Rewire Your Brain,
Regain Your Life

||||||||||||||||||||||||||||||||

*I don't have to chase extraordinary moments to find
happiness—it's right in front of me if I'm paying
attention and practicing gratitude.*

– BRENÉ BROWN

I was meeting with two new clients, Dr. Husband and Dr.
Wife, both MD-PhDs of psychiatry. My belly was truly sick
with nerves. These very busy doctors had sought me out for
a retirement plan, but how would they receive my opening
exercise, the Gratitude Exercise? After all, they came to me

for their bottom line, the "dollars and cents" of all they had accumulated, not a lesson in self-help.

The Gratitude Exercise had been referenced in the letter and email I'd sent prior to our meeting, but I have to assume the majority of new clients don't read these financial planning documents, since most don't allow themselves the luxury—especially two people this busy.

I felt a fool stepping into this meeting with my same tried-and-true process, but I did. *Begin in gratitude.*

Dr. Husband and Dr. Wife arrived a few minutes early. They were impeccably dressed, cordial but not overly warm—I suspect they weren't quite sure what the meeting might hold (and neither was I). Over a working lunch in a private room, I explained to them that day one of our engagement involved very little finance.

"Today is about identifying what you really, *really* want in life," I explained. "It's not a retirement plan or being financially secure. It's an all-encompassing picture of what is most dear to each of you individually. That picture is your Perfect Day, and the first step in crafting that picture is the Gratitude Exercise."

I gulped and paused to assess their gazes. All seemed okay—little to no reaction from either—so I proceeded.

I asked them to list ten things they were grateful for and the top five experiences they'd had in the last year. Once the lists were complete, I asked if either of them cared to share. Dr. Husband put down his fork and began.

What was to follow, I will never forget. Dr. Husband's posture changed; he was half bent over, gasping slightly for air. I started to move forward, as I thought he was choking on his lunch, but he wasn't. He was choked up in a different way—he was crying as a result of the Gratitude Exercise.

Dr. Husband regained his composure and read what he was grateful for. He shared that he'd never been asked to do an exercise like this and he said it really showed him all his many blessings and perhaps what he had been taking for granted. He was overwhelmed with appreciation for his wife, among other things.

In an instant, unknowingly, Dr. Husband had just redefined a part of my job description: moving clients to new depths of gratitude.

A new version of *my* Perfect Day emerged: it was no longer me climbing a mountain and celebrating with my kids after a successful seven-summit completion; it was a day at work with more Dr. Husbands and Dr. Wives, clients who were grateful for one another, and also grateful for a process I'd designed that turned traditional "retirement planning" on its head.

What retirement planning *should* look like is focusing your time, resources, and money on the things you are most grateful for: love, health, family, and, yes, travel, boats, and a mortgage-free house. But, as wise Dr. Covey said: First Things First.[2] Oh, and don't forget climbing those mountains.

The Happiest People On Earth

Bhutan is a small, landlocked country in the Eastern Himalayas. With a GDP of $6.83 billion, it is by no means a wealthy country. But did you know that the Bhutanese are the happiest people in the world?

There are a number of reasons for this. Maybe you have seen the list, "10 Things Bhutan People Do Differently That Make Them the Happiest People." It details the different aspects of the Bhutanese lifestyle that contribute to their overall well-being.[3]

Good habits and healthy practices with respect to consumption play a big role. For instance, the Bhutanese don't care about TV, radio, or the Internet. As a result, they are insulated from the envy, negativity, and addictions fueled by overexposure to media. They are not constantly comparing their situations with others. Nor do they develop an obsessive need to be connected.

---

2   Covey, Stephen R., Merrill, A. Roger, and Merrill, Rebecca R. First Things First (Simon & Schuster: 1994).

3   http://www.lifehack.org/articles/communication/8-things-bhutan-people-differently-that-make-them-the-happiest-people.html

Another important trait is their religion. The majority of people in Bhutan are Buddhist, a religion that emphasizes living good lives, doing good deeds, and being good people.

Environment matters, too. Over 50 percent of the country is protected as a national park. Having such care for living things and the land on which they live makes a difference in promoting quality of life. Moreover, the majority of the Bhutanese landscape is untouched wilderness. Having that kind of unfettered access to nature is important to refresh the body and the mind.

But to me, the single biggest reason that the Bhutanese are the happiest people on earth is that they are grateful. They're so grateful, they don't even think of themselves as grateful—gratitude has infused every fiber of their being. It's simply who they are.

How Can Gratitude Revolutionize Your Life?

One of my all-time favorite TED talks is by Shawn Achor, the CEO of Good Think Inc., where he researches and teaches about positive psychology. In his talk *The Happy Secret to Better Work,* Achor says, "Ninety percent of your long-term happiness is predicted not by the external world, but by the way your brain processes the world."[4]

Let's think about that for a moment. If 90 percent of our long-term happiness is *not* determined by our external environment, where we live, who we're surrounded by, our clothes, our car—well, then, we'd better get the inside *right*. But how?

It all starts with gratitude. The brain is wired to see the negative first. That's just human nature. But we can change that, simply by adding a two-minute gratitude exercise to our day.

Achor offers the following exercise: spend two minutes each day writing down three new things you are grateful for. After twenty-one days, *this actually changes the way your brain processes the world.* Your brain works more optimistically and has greater success at translating the external world into internal happiness. You are essentially training your brain to scan for positive things first.

We often think, "Once I get that promotion, I'll be happy" or "As soon as I find the right spouse, I'll feel optimistic again." But Achor says that's actually the *opposite* of how the

---

4   Achor, Shawn (May 2011). "The happy secret to better work." [Video file]. Retrieved from: https://www.ted.com/talks/shawn_achor_the_happy_secret_to_better_work

brain works. If you train the brain first instead of waiting for the world to drop a promotion or a spouse in your lap, things start to shift.

If you train your brain to think more positively, it will perform better—you'll be more intelligent and more creative, with more energy to implement new ideas. Achor has found that your brain at its positive best is 31 percent more productive than your brain at its negative worst.

We think success will make us happier, but we've got it backwards. If we work on happiness first, we'll experience more success. And one of the best ways to be more positive is to practice gratitude.

Achor mentions some of the traps our brain lays for us, including when we start to think happiness is "just beyond the horizon." This comes into play when I have clients design their Perfect Day. This exercise can be tricky—just when you think you've had such a day, the bar rises. Perfection, like the horizon, is never truly reachable: it's always a little bit farther from where you are.

This is why a critical part of Perfect Days is *mindset*. The foundation of the Perfect Day is not unattainable perfection; it's pure and simple gratitude. It is gratitude that will keep you stable, reminding you of what is real and important, of your progress and your blessings.

Do you have kids? Try this on for size. Our family keeps a large, white jar in the living room. Every day, before we go to bed, we take a piece of paper and jot down our name, the date, and three things we're thankful for and drop it in the jar. This is our way of "capturing" appreciation so that we can go back to the jar and reminisce. Thanksgiving, New Year's Day—these are great days for us to play "raffle" with our Jar of Thanks.

We haven't always had the Jar of Thanks. We started back in 2008 when Lee Brower, my business coach and the inspiration behind my entire financial planning process, start-to-finish, gave our family the idea of a gratitude rock. As I drove the girls to preschool, we'd pass the rock around and say what we were grateful for. Today, the rock sits on the island in our kitchen, almost a decade later, covered in kiddie stickers and worn with natural body oils. The rock reminds me of childlike innocence. Maybe we really do learn everything we need to know in kindergarten: "Hello, how are you?" "Please" and "Thanks." Simple thanks.

How do gratitude and the happiness quotient transfer over from our kids and families to the workplace? Achor's TED talk goes on to say that 75 percent of job success is *not* due to IQ, but is actually based on three key entrepreneurial skillsets: optimism, social support, and the ability to see stress as a challenge and not a threat. For me, the bedrock of these skills is gratitude.

Gratitude is where it all begins. Which explains why, when I work with new clients, we start with the Gratitude Exercise—the same exercise I'm now offering to you.

|||||||||||||||||||||||||||||||||||||||||||||||||||||||||||||||||||||||||||||||||||||||||||||||||||||||||||||||||||||||||||||||||||||||

SUGGESTED EXERCISE
Gratitude List and Top 5 Moments

Take out a fresh piece of paper and a pen or pencil. I want you to answer the following two prompts. No rules, no thinking—just write down the first thing that comes to mind.

With a pen or pencil, list out:

1. The ten things you are most thankful for
2. The five most positive experiences you've had in the last year.

Working through the Gratitude Exercise can be very powerful. Don't be afraid if it stirs up some deep emotions—Dr. Husband is not the only client who has cried while doing this exercise! It takes some time and honesty with yourself to do it properly, but I promise you, the rewards are well worth it.

Once you can identify what truly matters for you, the rest will dissipate. You will learn to separate the dirt from the gold in your priorities, which will carry over into your family, business, and investment strategies. The Gratitude Exercise will help you identify what's most important in your life now, which typically leads to a desire to create more of what you're grateful for: better health (smaller muffin top?!), better relationships, and sure, a well-oiled machine of a business that employs grateful and productive staffers.

Conversely, the Perfect Day trap could be a vision of a private jet that takes you to Machu Picchu with your kids—but if you're not healthy enough to hike to the top and if your kids really don't care to be around you, well, that trip to Peru not only just got really expensive, it also just turned into the *worst day ever*. Catch my drift?

If this exercise was meaningful to you, I encourage you to incorporate it into your daily routine. Jot down three things you are grateful for every day, or if that's too hard to maintain, write out ten things you are grateful for on a regular basis. Every time you do this, go back in time to answer the second question. What has happened over the last twelve months that were positive experiences? Trips? Hitting revenue goals? Hitting personal goals? A new employee? New relationships? All of these experiences are part of the Perfect Day recipe, too.

CHAPTER 5

Step Two:
Asset Inventory and Vision Focuser

||||||||||||||||||||||||||||||

"Measure your wealth not by the things you have, but by the things for which you would not take money."
–DAVE RAMSEY, FINANCIAL PEACE REVISITED

As we've established, the Perfect Day concept is not my genius creation. You may have already heard of it, or a similar strategy built on the same ideas. I'm often quoted as saying, "It's not my wheel—I just make the wheel mine."

The Perfect Day approach I created owes much to my life coach, Claire Stuhr, but it is also inspired by another one of my coaches and mentor, Lee Brower, whom I mentioned in Chapter 4. I consider this book to be a trifecta, the collaborative cocktail of Claire's legacy, Lee's brilliance, and my everyday client-application knowledge: a potent prescription for any entrepreneur experiencing Lifestyle Deficit Disorder.

Before we discuss Asset Inventory and Vision Focuser, I want to talk a little about Lee. His work has transformed the way I do business, and moreover, the way I live my life. His strategies and methodologies have galvanized my Perfect Day approach, and I like to think I've been able to integrate his philosophy by building off it and making it my own.

Lee Brower is part finance genius and part spiritual guru—he wouldn't agree on the guru part, but he *is*. He is the creator and author of *The Brower Quadrant* and the concept of Empowered Wealth®. Over the years, his core message has remained refreshingly consistent: gratitude, gratitude, gratitude.

Lee's breakthrough vision was this: while most of us are concerned with transferring our financial wealth to the next generation, we should be more focused on transferring our most important assets, something he calls "core assets."

These assets include our family values, our health, and our belief system.

Go back to your Gratitude list—how many of the items listed were financial in nature? *Aha!* Typically, what we're most thankful for aren't financial in nature, but more core-centric. Don't get me wrong: we're not in business for ourselves for the gray hair. We work hard so that, ultimately, we have money—and hopefully, lots of it!

But as you may now see, this is the genesis of putting you before your business: fitting your business and all that it needs around you and you core assets, not the other way around. Our core assets form the foundation of the eponymous quadrants in *The Brower Quadrant*. So when I say Lee wrote the book on quadrant living ... well, he did.

Lee's exercise of identifying your assets and categorizing them into quadrants is one I've made integral to crafting your Perfect Day. As an Empowered Wealth Ambassador™, I continue to use this philosophy and have found it to be the most effective way of inventorying a client's assets to determine where her time, attention, and resources should be spent in order to achieve the best outcomes.

Guess what? Your assets aren't always what you think they are—and they're not always *where* you think they are, either.

Inventory Time! (Don't worry—this is an inventory task you'll like.)

When I meet a new client, the first thing I do, after the initial Gratitude Exercise, is take them through an asset inventory.

"Tell me about your asset—no rules, no definitions," I say.

Some people ask, "Well what do you mean 'asset?' Are you talking about my money?"

At this point, I explain they are free to define the word however they see fit. Sure, some of those assets will be financial—but not all.

One thing I love about Lee's quadrants is that they are easy and intuitive. Using his philosophy, all your assets can be divided into the following four groups:

1. **CORE assets:** family, health, values, You-ness, relationships, heritage, religion/spirituality, ethics

These are the most important assets—as I mentioned, there's probably a lot of crossover with the results of your Gratitude Exercise. Core assets I often see are health, children, and faith.

2. **EXPERIENCE assets:** wisdom, education, ideas, world-view, acquired skills/talents, traditions, good/bad

experiences, places you've traveled to, alliances you've forged, networks, associations.

These include a person's training, education, skills, networks, and the places they have traveled. Here's something to keep in mind: more often than not, the best experience assets are your worst experiences, not your best ones! What life lessons have you learned from mistakes made, whether in business or your personal life? How can you make more of that asset? These are the hard life lessons that shaped you into who you are today. I'd call those valuable assets.

3. **CONTRIBUTION assets:** anonymous actions that better mankind, volunteerism, charitable contributions of time and money, private foundations, etc. These are "gratitude"-based assets. The real question here is, "What are you doing to empower others without really expecting anything in return?" And, yes, this does include the proactive management of your taxes to make sure you are optimizing the use of your financial assets.

Your approach to your taxes is representative of your desire to take control of those dollars that can be wisely used to benefit society in ways you choose, while still being supportive as a citizen of our nation. You can choose to prudently pay less to the IRS through pro-active tax planning strategies.

4. **FINANCIAL** **assets:** cash, stocks and bonds, retirement accounts, businesses, real estate, other material possessions—this one you get, right?

Now that you know the four classes, take a few minutes to complete the following exercise.

1. Make a list of your twenty most important assets. These could include your house, boat, 401(k), your education, your church—anything. There are no rules as to what an asset is: if it's important to you, it's an asset. If it makes you grateful, it's an asset. (HINT: You can use the answers from your Gratitude Exercise at the end of Chapter 4 to add to your asset list.)

2. Add a second column to the right, and beside each asset, write: Core, Experience, Contribution, or Financial.

I'm going to share with you what this list looks like for a client who recently came to see me.

perfect day ◆ asset inventory

ASSETS	ASSET CLASS
1. House	Financial
2. 401k	Financial
3. Family	Core
4. Health	Core
5. Children	Core
6. Education	Experience
7. Travel	Experience
8. Church/ Faith	Core
9. Business	Financial
10. Divorce/ Child Custody	Experience
11. Mission Work	Contribution
12. Inheritance	Financial
13. Secure Job	Financial
14. Family Values	Core
15. Pension	Financial
16. Getting Sober	Experience
17. Family Endowment	Contribution
18. Business Colleagues	Experience
19. Friends	Core
20. Volunteer Work	Contribution

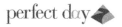

Sometimes when I do this exercise, the client is still thinking of "asset" as "financial," so the vast majority of their assets fall into that category. But this client is a little more balanced, with six core assets, five experience assets, three contribution assets, and six financial assets.

There's no right or wrong answer to your Asset Inventory. All you have to do is list out the things that are most important to you. After all, that's what an asset is: something of value to you.

Watching people inventory their assets makes for an interesting human experiment. Men will frequently respond with financially tangible assets. They might say, "Well, I've got a boat. I've got a house. I've got a 401(k)." Women, on the other hand, will tend to list those things you can't itemize on a tax form. They might say, "I have my children, my health, and my faith in God."

Many clients have told me that some of their best experience assets come from their worst experiences. It's been true for me, too. Before I left big brokerage and set out on my own, I was part of a business partnership. Long story short: after waging a gender discrimination and retaliation suit against my employer and former partner, I left the partnership and lost a ton of capital in the way of clients. It was the worst legal and financial battle of my life, and an almost total reset on my career and client base. I was faced with starting over, but at the same time, I was unknowingly in the heat of creating my own best experiences—standing up for myself and for what was right. It was the best gift my career could have been given.

At the time, this development seemed like a tremendous loss. But ultimately, it was a win—a win for values, and a win for learning how to stand up for myself. That horrible experience turned out to be a positive experience asset. It resulted in my own growth, both personally and professionally. It led to me walking away from a big practice and going into business for myself. It also set an example for my two daughters that it's worth it to stand up for yourself, especially as a woman in the workplace.

I didn't care about the money or what I'd lost, because my values were more important. I wasn't going to stand by and let myself be devalued. I've never looked back—and today, things have never looked better.

What difficult or painful experiences in your life count as experience assets? Have you had to walk away from business partnerships? Ended friendships or marriages? Lost people who were dear to you? Battled health challenges? Gone through periods of great financial stress or bankruptcy? While these experiences may have been hard, they've also made you richer. These are your experience assets, your battle scars, the hardships and battles and victories that have helped make you who you are today.

Now that you've inventoried your assets, we turn our attention to the Vision Focuser.

Focus Your Vision

This next exercise is called the Vision Focuser because it will be the cornerstone of focusing your vision on the right things. It's going to help you remember what you really, really, really want for your Perfect Day.

Sometimes the Perfect Day exercise can go off the rails when a client says they want to spend the day on their own personal jet or staring into their closetful of hundreds of pairs of designer shoes (actual examples!). This is why I direct clients to write down their *twenty most important assets*. The client whose Perfect Day includes a closetful full of new shoes didn't list her shoes on her Top Twenty asset inventory, so shoes would never make the cut for her Perfect Day. The same goes for the overachiever who wanted the jet. (He got his jet, by the way—but only after he refocused his core vision!)

Before I perfected this exercise, the jet and the shoes snuck into the Perfect Day and sometimes caused clients to strive for the wrong things. The things—assets—we have now, for the most part, are all we need. But we can make these assets better: better health, better relationships, more volunteer work, a bigger 401(k). The Vision Focuser will force you to inventory your most important assets and then identify which assets you are lacking—and then which assets you wish to make the focus your time, attention, and resources.

The strength of your vision is going to help you achieve the things that are truly the most important. No one has ever listed a Lexus or their Louis Vuitton collection among the "most important" assets—not yet, anyway!

To help you zero in on the most important things, I created the Perfect Day Pyramid.

A pyramid is a powerful shape, one of the strongest shapes in geometry. With its broad, steady base, it is able to support massive amounts of weight. The ancient Egyptians sometimes spent ten years or more building a single pyramid. Luckily, this exercise is not going to take you that long!

For me, pyramids symbolize hard work and dedication to build something magnificent and beautiful—something that lasts.

When I use this model with new clients, I put their most prized asset category—those all-important Core assets—into the heart of the pyramid. Think of these assets as "royalty;" after all, the Egyptians built the pyramids as tombs for their great kings!

The other three asset classes go on the pyramid's sides:

The Vision Focuser

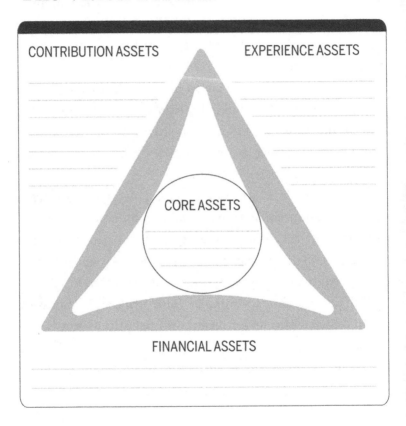

CONTRIBUTION ASSETS

EXPERIENCE ASSETS

CORE ASSETS

FINANCIAL ASSETS

perfect day

Here's how the Vision Focuser looked for my new client:

The Vision Focuser

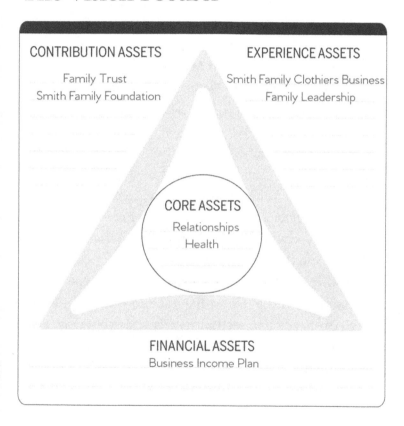

CONTRIBUTION ASSETS

Family Trust
Smith Family Foundation

EXPERIENCE ASSETS

Smith Family Clothiers Business
Family Leadership

CORE ASSETS

Relationships
Health

FINANCIAL ASSETS
Business Income Plan

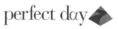

||||||||||||||||||||||||||||||||||||||||||||||||||||||||||||||||||||||||||||

Zen is the spirit of the valley, not the
mountaintop. The only Zen you'll find on
the tops of mountains is the Zen you bring
up there."

–ROBERT M. PIRSIG

ZEN AND THE ART OF MOTORCYCLE MAINTENANCE

||||||||||||||||||||||||||||||||||||||||||||||||||||||||||||||||||||||||||||

Plotting out your assets on the Perfect Day Pyramid
creates a powerful visual. Now you can see the areas where
you've invested yourself—your time, energy, resources,
passion—and reflect on whether those investments are in
line with the person, businessperson or otherwise, who you
want to be and the lifestyle you want to have.

But what if, after you do the above exercise, you see that
one section of the pyramid has far more assets than the
others? Or maybe one section has *fewer* assets—maybe you
have nine financial assets, but only three core assets. What
happens then?

This is when we encounter something Lee Brower calls a
"wobble."

What's Your Wobble?

Imagine you're driving down the highway. You're
traveling appropriately at sixty-five to seventy miles per

hour. Suddenly, a big SUV veers into your lane, and you have to swerve to avoid hitting it.

The level of balance in your tires directly correlates to how you recover from the swerve. If you swerve and two of your tires are underinflated, the likelihood of you rolling your car into a ditch and experiencing death or permanent disability is high. The accident could have lasting effects—it could lead to long-term injury or a heart attack. It could put strain on your marriage and increase your risk of divorce. You might have to face all sorts of potentially bad consequences, all because those two tires were underinflated.

It's the same with life. Once you understand what your four key asset categories contain, the next step is to make sure they are all balanced. If you've been neglecting or overemphasizing one or more asset categories, you're left with a "wobble," not unlike what you would experience driving a car with one or more underinflated or overinflated tires. And wobbles can be dangerous.

If you don't have a wobble because all tires are equally balanced, then when you swerve out of the way of that SUV, it's a non-event. You recover. The car doesn't roll or spin out of control. Maybe you sigh, or you brandish your hand at the careless driver and shout a choice swear word. Maybe you simply sigh. But you emerge unscathed. You are okay.

When you have a wobble and a crisis happens, the wobble intensifies the crisis. When everything is balanced, a crisis hits and you move right through it. Not only does it not leave a scar—it doesn't even leave a scratch.

Wobbles result in imbalanced results in life, usually toward the negative side. If your health is in check and there's no wobble, and you trip and fall down a flight of stairs, the chances of the event being a non-event or a speedy recovery are good. I say this from personal experience: I've had two big falls over the last few years. I've been juggling six different bags and a cup of coffee and fallen down stairs without breaking a hip or blowing out my knee. Like I tell my clients, "That's why you work out!"

But let's get serious. Take the following example: your business processes are all in check and your staff is dutifully and productively on task—and then you lose your biggest account. If you don't have a wobble, you've got the financial assets to stay on target and the experience assets to connect you with other big contracts that will keep your business afloat. If you have a wobble, you aren't going to be able to right yourself nearly as swiftly and efficiently—and you might capsize altogether.

More relevant today—and a huge culprit to those suffering from acute LDD—is the wobble in our relationships. Ever heard of the "bank account of life" concept? Make more deposits than you do withdrawals? When your business comes first and your core assets—your most prized possessions—*don't* come first, a crisis might send you into being overdrawn. This is a recipe for the life lesson you never wanted. It's a wobble from which you can recover, but only if you inflate that tire *today*. Not tomorrow, but today.

It's all about balance. If your assets are out of balance, you risk a blowout or worse. But if all four tires are in good working order, equilibrium will be restored, meaning you'll be able to drive safely and smoothly again.

When I work with clients, the single most effective way to "find the wobble" is to lead them in an affirmations exercise as a way to help them refine and refocus their goals. In the next chapter, you'll affirm what is most important to you. Then we'll use those affirmations to get you back behind the steering wheel, with better balanced tires, en route to your Perfect Day.

CHAPTER 6

Step Three: Affirmations and Perfect Day Vision

||||||||||||||||||||||||||||||

Being the richest man in the cemetery doesn't matter to me. Going to bed at night saying we've done something wonderful ... that's what matters to me.

–STEVE JOBS

As you career from one subpar day to the next, what are you sacrificing? What are you giving up? And is it ultimately worth it?

When the focus of human beings is placed in core values, sustainable happiness becomes possible. On the other hand, when emphasis is placed on financial assets, life goes out the window and LDD takes hold.

Think about it: when you are fixated on a dollar value and believe that that number holds the key to your happiness kingdom, you become preoccupied with the wrong things. You get obsessed with not losing that amount. You feel the pressure to maintain a certain numerical level of earnings, and you spiral into thoughts like, "What if I don't hit my revenue targets? What if I don't get the contract or the client?"

One casualty in this rat race is sleep. Sleep is supremely important to feeling refreshed and vital to your physical and mental well-being, yet we do not get nearly enough sleep.

I'm guilty of this. I'm someone who has been saying for years that I do really well on five to six hours of sleep. But now all the studies coming out are showing that brain clarity, brain function, and productivity are quite poor at that level. Arianna Huffington's recently released *The Sleep Revolution* was a byproduct of the media mogul's own case of LDD.[5] When Huffington woke up one morning in a pool of blood, she realized she'd collapsed from lack of sleep and shattered

---

5   Barron, James. New York Times. "Not Sleeping Enough? Arianna Huffington Wants to Help," December 4, 2016. http://www.nytimes. com/2016/12/04/nyregion/not-sleeping-enough-arianna-huffington-wants-to-help.html

her cheekbone when she fell. For two years, she'd been working eighteen-hour days to build the Huffington Post—one of the most widely read websites in the United States. But success had come at a cost.

Huffington asserts a bold claim: in our hyper-connected society, when we are all expected to be "plugged in" twenty-four hours a day to our cell phones and computers, we are suffering from a worldwide epidemic of sleeplessness. We think that, if we want to experience success, we have to overwork, under-sleep, and burn the candle at both ends. But by doing so, ultimately we burn out.

Remember Bhutan, the happiest place in the world? Number nine on the list of lifestyle habits of the Bhutanese is that they are well-rested. This feeds into their overall well-being. They are well-rested because they're not anxious about anything! They are not stuck in traffic. They're not commuting. They're not sitting with screens in front of them all the time. They're not keeping up with the Joneses. They're in nature, practicing their faith, enjoying life.

If monetary wealth is all that you are after, then you are in good company. But be forewarned, money won't bring you happiness. As a matter of fact, in many cases, money will *cost* you happiness. Intuitively, you know this.

If overall happiness is what you're seeking, then you need to invest in a different kind of life plan, one rooted in core values and nurturing balance among your critical assets. The framework to cure LDD and stay on a path of LDD remission is right within your grasp. The plan is the Perfect Day Pyramid.

One is never "cured" of LDD. You don't go into remission and never worry about it again. We must always be connected to the idea that LDD could be lingering right around the corner, and we must remain ever-vigilant so that we don't let our former lifestyle sneak back in.

Everyone's Perfect Day is very personal—I can't tell you what yours entails. What I *can* tell you is that an integral component of any Perfect Day is personal and professional growth, in tandem with gratitude.

So how do you craft a day like that? By keeping your eyes on the prize—and finding the places you need to grow.

Keeping Your Eyes on the Prize

Most entrepreneurs and non-entrepreneurs alike have enough time, but lack the vision. Take Patrick, a brilliant young tech guy working eighty hours a week to launch his startup. He's actively growing his company and he has a prestigious MBA and all sorts of business connections—but he hardly ever sees his wife or newborn baby, and he certainly doesn't have the time to do service work. His core and contribution assets are nearing overdrawn in the bank account of life. We can safely assume that his gratitude and an attitude of giving back—wanting to leave this world a better place than he found it—are low or maybe nonexistent.

"So what?" you might ask. "He's working hard. He'll get to the other stuff later, but right now, he's growing his business. He can't have high core and contribution assets *all* the time."

It's true that our assets may shift from time to time; there is a certain level of fluidity in the Vision Focuser, wherein some classes may see greater or fewer assets in any given month or year. But your core assets shouldn't really change.

In Patrick's case, he is missing out on valuable time with his family, especially during the first few critical years of his son's life. And if he is chronically low on contribution assets, that's problematic, too. Two of his tires are seriously over-inflated, and two of them are underinflated, leading to a pretty severe wobble. That's going to zap his energy, passion, joy, and zest for getting out of bed every day.

What about you? When you reflect on your core, experience, contribution, and financial assets we identified in the Vision Focuser, where do you see an opportunity for growth?

Take out your Perfect Day Pyramid from Chapter 5. Looking at your four asset classes, ask yourself the following two questions:

1. Which area(s) are you strongest in?
2. Which area(s) are you weakest in?

Another way of asking these questions is: Where are your assets heavy, and where are they light?

3. In each asset category, identify **one asset** that you'd like to multiply, make bigger, or have more of.
4. Go through and **circle these assets**. You should have a total of **four**.

Let's say health is one of your core assets. You might say, "My financial assets—my boat, my pension, my business—they're all doing great. My experience assets are awesome: I have three degrees from top-notch universities and I've visited over three-dozen countries. I have over a million followers on Twitter. And I give back to various charities and do 200 hours of volunteer work every year.

"But I'm out of shape. I've just had a cardiac bypass. I want to get healthier."

It might feel indulgent to say, "I want the first thing I do every day to be a forty-five-minute workout, because I value my health. I want to feel good." But it isn't indulgent at all. Without your health, you won't feel rich, no matter how much you have in your portfolio.

Let's look at an example from one of my clients:

The Vision Focuser

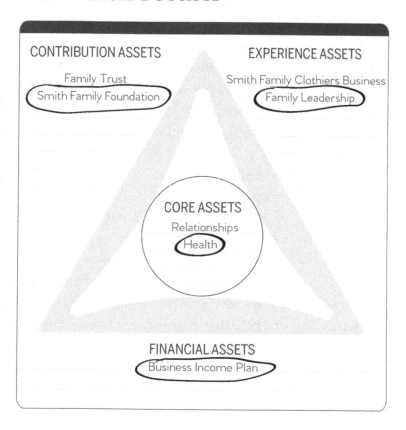

CONTRIBUTION ASSETS

Family Trust
Smith Family Foundation

EXPERIENCE ASSETS

Smith Family Clothiers Business
Family Leadership

CORE ASSETS

Relationships
Health

FINANCIAL ASSETS

Business Income Plan

When you complete this exercise, you should emerge with a clear focus on four areas where you want to focus greater time, energy, and resources. These areas of development are your Perfect Day activities—and then some.

Ever have those moments where you look up and say, "I have so much to do—where do I even start?" When you feel overwhelmed, take a step toward any one of your areas of development. If it's exercise, text your trainer and book an appt. Contribution assets need work? Email or make a quick call to your CPA for a tax review—or call your charity of choice to see where their greatest area of need is. Financial? Scan your business operations file and decide what expense you're cutting, or call your most important client "just because." This way, most of your days are getting closer to ... well, perfect.

While the core assets are obviously important, please don't think that you can't also desire—and experience—growth in one of the other three asset classes. You can absolutely set financial goals! In 2015, a client of mine wanted to achieve a greater level of liquidity in his net worth. One of his areas of focus over the coming years was centered on business and personal decisions that created cash and more readily available assets in his life.

Three years later, he achieved it. What was once a real-estate-heavy, non-marketable, business-stock-heavy financial picture led to a purchase offer, and today my client has a fully liquid portfolio.

Other clients have identified health and wellness as an area of focus: they want to get more exercise. So they join a gym, complete marathons, or climb mountains to shed that muffin top. Before, any of those things would have been the dreaded antichrist; now they want to do them as an activity on their Perfect Day. See the shift?

Affirmations Exercise

Positive affirmations go a long way in turning a challenge into a victory. If you live in fear of the four things circled on your list, or if you view them as a source of negativity—"I'm never going to pay off my mortgage" or "I'm overweight and there's nothing I can do about it"—then you're robbing yourself of an exciting opportunity for growth and positive change.

To turn your asset deficits into your Perfect Day activities, use the following worksheet to complete this simple exercise:

1. Look at the four items you want more of. Write four sentences in present tense, but imagine yourself saying these things a year from today. Write them as if the sentence were true: "I saved enough to pay off my mortgage," or "I ran a marathon in under

five hours, injury free." Choose true, specific, and measureable affirmations.

perfect day asset inventory

ASSETS	ASSET CLASS
1. House	Financial
2. 401k	Financial
3. Family	Core
4. Health	Core
5. Children	Core
6. Education	Experience
7. Travel	Experience
8. Church/ Faith	Core
9. Business	Financial
10. Divorce/ Child Custody	Experience
11. Mission Work	Contribution
12. Inheritance	Financial
13. Secure Job	Financial
14. Family Values	Core
15. Pension	Financial
16. Getting Sober	Experience
17. Family Endowment	Contribution
18. Business Colleagues	Experience
19. Friends	Core
20. Volunteer Work	Contribution

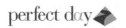

2. Find the right location. When you pick your spot, I suggest you choose somewhere quiet and serene. Ideally, it will be somewhere you'd like to spend time on your Perfect Day. It could be a local Starbucks, or it could be a beach in Tahiti—but do you see the trouble with Tahiti? It's hard to have more than a couple of those days a year. If you cultivate appreciation for the everyday spots, like a sacred park bench or the corner booth in Starbucks near the electric outlet, you can almost have 365 Perfect Days a year. So choose someplace like that and set yourself up for success.

3. Now your job is to transform these statements into your Perfect Day in full, written form. Take your four positive affirmations and mold them into a story that, one year from now, is *true*. In addition to your four sentences, describe where you are on your Perfect Day—what you're wearing, how you feel, who you are with—all with a dose of gratitude. Tell a story: how does your day begin? What do you do for lunch? Who is with you as the sun goes down? Let the story flow out of you, and let your dream be as big and as wild as your heart desires. *This* is your Perfect Day.

To further inspire you, here is an example of how one of my clients plotted out her Perfect Day:

perfect day

Today is a perfect day. I begin my day by:

Today I woke up early without an alarm feeling refreshed and energized. I feel spiritually centered, optimistic about the day and ready to handle anything that comes my way with ease. I have more than enough time to make a healthy breakfast after a 60-minute yoga session with my private instructor. I eat my fresh eggs and fruit outside in my beautiful garden with my husband, with the sun shining brightly, as we discuss upcoming travel plans.

After breakfast, I meet with my book publisher to talk about upcoming promotions; the book is awesome and I am so proud of the piece it developed into. Mid-day I get an email from my doctor with a glowing report of my health stats—I am indeed healthier than I have been in my whole life; I feel great, I look great and I feel mentally strong and clear, too. "I know I can" is a regular phrase I have retrained myself to say and profess as I tackle daily challenges, big and small.

The girls and I are scheduled to volunteer at 180 Place later this afternoon and it has become a routine that we look forward to. The Smith Family Foundation annual meeting is later this quarter and will fund our biggest year of giving, to date. We are proud of our giving and how we are supporting our community and the girls have become fantastic examples to their peers.

My Budget for Conscience living is complete and has become a seamless part of my finances. I enjoy abiding by it and we even used it today in our discussion of future travel. My day ends with a bubble bath while googling family activities to do in the Galapagos this Christmas. Life is good, what a Perfect Day.

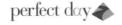

You know you've achieved the Perfect Day when you feel a sense of freedom. You're free to do what you wish— and you are *choosing* to spend your day intentionally in the direction of personal growth. No one is forcing you to run that marathon: you're choosing to!

||||||||||||||||||||||||||||||

PART FOUR
Implementing Your Perfect Day: How to Make Commander's Intent, Your You-ness, Time, Energy, and Delegation Work for You

||||||||||||||||||||||||||||||

If your success is not on your own terms,
if it looks good to the world but does not
feel good in your heart, it is not success
at all.

–ANNA QUINDLEN

CHAPTER 7

Crafting Your Commander's Intent

||||||||||||||||||||||||||||||||

Don't tell people how to do things, tell them what to do and let them surprise you with their results.
–General George S. Patton

I n the late '80s and early '90s, the U.S. Army came up with a system called the "Commander's Intent." It was created in order to help soldiers strategize around events beyond the control or anticipation of army leaders.

For example, during World War II, the commander would be in charge of providing detailed instructions to his platoon in order to complete their mission. He might say, "Here we are at Point A. You are charged with taking the hill, which is Point B—and here's how you're going to do it: Go fifty clicks to the west, cross a bridge, and then continue twenty clicks to the east."

The problem was that the platoon members were not given much latitude to exercise their own judgment. They were not empowered to make decisions. They were told, "These are your specific directives." This is fine when things go well, but what happens when they go fifty clicks to the west and see that the bridge they're supposed to cross has been booby-trapped? They were not left with much recourse, only with the question, "What do we do now?"

To address this dilemma, the U.S. Army came up with a concept called "Commander's Intent." The objective of this was to empower platoon members. With the Commander's Intent (CI) in place, in the same scenario as above, the commander would say to his subordinates, "You are at Point A, and we want you to take the hill, which is Point B. We don't care how you do it, but here are rules: don't kill any women, children, or unarmed soldiers. Your mission: Take the hill."

In this way, that platoon is carrying out exactly what their commanders wanted, but when they come to the bridge that is booby-trapped, they can make their own decisions on how to proceed—so long as they follow the guidelines set forth by their superiors.

An Operating Manual for Your Life

The Commander's Intent has left an indelible mark on my life and those of my clients. In Chapter 5, we identified our assets. Included in those assets were our core values: what we truly believe and desire. If we want to transform that Perfect Day from a static worksheet into a living, breathing reality, we need to first come up with a mission statement that captures the very essence of our deepest values.

That's what the Commander's Intent is for.

I firmly believe that if you come up with a mission statement that is well-formed, then just about any decision in your life can be tested against it. If it passes, then you know you're headed in the right direction. Think of it as an operating manual for not only your business, but your life. You can and should have several CIs to guide the various aspects of your life: family, business, personal, project-specific, and so-on.

This has been proven true in my own family. My husband and I came up with a statement about seven years ago for the four of us: Tony, our two girls, and me. Ours is, "We choose us, and that which energizes us." That's our Commander's Intent. We can allow many situations to pass through that filter, and this provides us with the answers to many important questions.

For instance, we may have people come and ask us for money. And then we think about it. "We choose us, and that which energizes us." Sometimes it feels good to give people money and help them out. But you know what? It doesn't really energize me when the person comes back to me and wants to borrow more money, when they've not paid back what they owed in the first place. That does not give me energy. It does not make me feel good. So the answer in that instance would be no.

It also spills over into decisions regarding which clients I accept. If I know I'm going to have a high-maintenance client who will drain me and not send me home at the end of the day with energy for my family, I don't choose that client.

In *Made to Stick: Why Some Ideas Survive and Others Die*, the Heath brothers offer a powerful example of a simple, effective, and profitable CI: that of Southwest Airlines. "Southwest has a Commander's Intent, a core, that helps to guide this coordination. As related by James Carville and Paul Begala: Herb Kelleher (the longest-serving CEO of Southwest) once told someone, 'I can teach you the secret to running this airline in thirty seconds. This is it: We are THE low-fare airline. Once you understand that fact, you can make any decision about this company's future as well as I can.

"'Here's an example,' he said. 'Tracy from marketing comes into your office. She says her surveys indicate that the passengers might enjoy a light entrée on the Houston to Las Vegas flight. All we offer is peanuts, and she thinks a nice chicken Caesar salad would be popular. What do you say?' The person stammered for a moment, so Kelleher responded: 'You say, "Tracy, will adding that chicken Caesar salad make us THE low-fare airline from Houston to Las Vegas? Because if it doesn't help us become the unchallenged low-fare airline, we're not serving any damn chicken salad."'

The CI devised by Herb Kelleher is deceptive in its simplicity: "We are THE low-fare airline." Simple as it may be, those five words are unbelievably powerful. That little statement has fueled Southwest's great success by guiding every employee's actions, big or small, for more than thirty years.

A Powerful Tool for Fostering Collaboration

The right Commander's Intent—especially in the context of a business, specific project, or a partnership—can be particularly effective in maximizing collaboration. Without the CI, what happens inevitably is that individuals end up making unilateral decisions, even when they are part of a family or a company. Ultimately, this has an impact on the unity within the partnership.

Another way to think about this is to understand the Commander's Intent as a form of "common language" shared by you and your closest associates. This can refer to your spouse, your colleagues, and your employees, as well as your clients. Articulating the values you hold most dear—and having your clients and associates do the same for you—will make collaborations go more smoothly and stay more in line with the values of all parties involved. Throw out the company mission statement in lieu of a concise, pithy CI that is impenetrable.

For instance, without our family's Commander's Intent, Tony may decide to take on a client because it's an incredibly high-paying job that takes him to Poland—but it may not serve the rest of the family. It may not energize us. It may not be choosing us. And "us" here refers to the *four* of us—not the two of us, or just one of us.

When it comes to my professional life, I make sure there are clearly defined Commander's Intents established with my clients, so that I can be empowered to be the platoon: that is, I become the platoon for my clients. They may come to me and say, "I have a new business opportunity that involves fully staffed multiple locations, with a fantastic ROI of 18 percent per year." Knowing already that this client's CI is "Simplify," I have my answer for them. If their CI was "All investments earn 15 percent-plus" the opportunity would be a GO!

Now that, of course, is a simplistic example, but hopefully it illustrates how these CI's can work. They've empowered me to collaborate with and make the best decisions on behalf of my clients.

What a Well-Crafted Commander's Intent Can Do for You

The Commander's Intent came into my practice as a guideline for making decisions about finances. I had clients who didn't want to own certain stocks—maybe in alcohol or tobacco. Or they wanted to ensure that they were being socially responsible with their investments. In other instances, a client might come to me and say, "I just got an inheritance. What do I do with the money?" When we sit down together and craft a strong CI, it becomes a kind of guiding mantra.

Over the years, I have come across a number of great Commander's Intents. One in particular that comes to mind is the "Freedom to choose," which was the CI for my client John. John would fully admit to getting easily tantalized by new and exciting, shiny baubles, which often made it difficult for him to meet his financial goals. One day John came to me and said, "I want the new Tesla Roadster. It's a hundred thousand dollars, but I think I should treat myself." Because there was a properly crafted CI in place, I was able to respond, "John, two years ago, when we created your Commander's Intent, the most important thing to you and your family was to get debt-free and pay off your mortgage. Does getting a Tesla Roadster allow you to do that?"

It was clear that John purchasing the Tesla would not be in keeping with the CI "Freedom to choose." That car would not give John a debt-free retirement, but paying off his mortgage would. For John, "Freedom to choose" meant his family living within their means. It meant freedom to choose to work or *not* work. As I told John, "If you have a Tesla but still have a mortgage payment, I'd say your retirement dollars are smaller than if you'd bought the used Lexus!"

Another example of a CI comes from my own family's experience. My husband is an industrial engineer, and during the Great Recession of 2008-2009, manufacturing in this country shut down—it just came to a screeching halt. Despite this, my husband chose to not lay off any employees.

The stress of that payroll, and the stress of having to meet this obligation when there was no income to support it, was a situation that led us to craft our Commander's Intent of "We choose us and that which energizes us." We now had a framework for how we would make independent decisions at our own respective businesses in a way that honored one another and our family.

To develop your Commander's Intent, you must first answer the question: what do you really want? Sounds simple, but it takes a lot of soul-searching to arrive at the right answer. And yet, consider the alternative: what happens if you go the rest of your life without knowing the answer to this question?

Consider your wobble. Even if executed at only 50 percent, this should give you the answer to what you really, really want. It may not be self-evident now, but I urge you to go through the motions, balance your wobble, and bask in the outcome.

How to Craft Your Commander's Intent

A Commander's Intent is slightly different from a traditional mission statement. The most effective CIs are a short phrase versus your typical two-sentence mission statement.

You start by simply asking the question: What do you want your time, effort, and resources to bring you in the next year? Month? Day? A CI can be situational—project-based—or broad-life-based. A sign of a good broad-life-based CI is one that is timeless and will never change. This CI will travel with you wherever you go. We grow and our lives change, but our values and core beliefs do not. My personal CI, "Be who you admire," hasn't changed in twelve years. I'd be so proud if it were my epitaph: "Cokie's true north was to emulate the best attributes of those she admired yet never seek to be admired herself."

Imagine you wake up and it's one year later from today's date. What has to be true for you to be over the moon? What would you have to attain, achieve, or reach to feel that elated?

By this point, you'll have gone through your Vision Focuser exercise and outlined your Perfect Day to ensure that you're not chasing some elusive goal (i.e., the private jet) that's going to require a seventy-hour workweek. I'm asking what you *really* want.

Here's another way to look at it: you've been given one year to live. What needs to be true on the 366th day, when you die? Your CI should be a filter for all activities over the next 365 days. If they don't pass the CI filter of getting you closer to dying actualized on day 366, then it's not an effective CI.

You can have a CI for your family, business, staff, a particular project, and so forth. In fact, you *should* have separate CIs for all those listed. Try to include inspiration, plausibility, and specificity. Again, an effective CI is short and memorable, and it should contain what you consider a value proposition to you. If you were a buyer, what would sell you? More time? More energy? I'll warn you: more money is a trap. It's better to ask yourself *why* you want more money.

I never give clients examples of CI's, because it tends to lead them; they say, "Oh, I like that one!" NOPE. You can't get off that easy. But alas, the purpose of this book is to guide you to the Perfect Day and put you into perpetual remission from LDD. You're going to need a CI to help keep you and your business and your family in a place to support your health and well-being, and to help you shun the negative voices that say you can't do it.

So, going against my own best practice, here are some of my favorite custom CIs. I should note that I mean "custom" to *other* clients; you should strive to create a custom CI for yourself. If you don't come up with one overnight, that's a good sign. Sit with one and let it marinate. Test it when your gut gives you the feeling that you're engaging in an activity that won't get you where you want to be. It may take weeks or months, but commit to crafting a timeless CI.

The first two are ones I've already mentioned:

- "We choose us and that which energizes us." **Family CI** (all financial, time, and effort decisions support energy and positivity; good-fit clients; productive, on-board employees; exercise, healthy eating, and energy-building habits, etc.).
- "Freedom to choose." **Retirement plan CI** (all financial, time, and effort decisions support the

freedom to choose to work or to retire—liquidity, debt reduction, expense reduction—all supporting quitting TODAY).

- "Write my story." **Overall CI** (all financial, time, and effort decisions must support family legacy and telling the story of the family business).

- "Be who I admire." **Overall CI** (all financial, time, and effort decisions must be funneled into being someone I admire).

"Don't Make It Too Broad"

Good Commander's Intents (CI's) are simple yet specific and can be applied to a multitude of situations with the same good results: helping you arrive at your desired outcome according to the values you hold most dear.

This cannot happen, however, if your CI's are too broad or too complicated. I remember a client who came up with F.A.M.I.L.Y. as their Commander's Intent. Each letter stood for some kind of principle or maxim while collectively spelled out "family," reminding the client to always put family first.

The problem with this mantra was that it was far too broad to be effective. It was too permissive and therefore allowed too many decisions to pass through. Moreover, it was too much work to remember what all those letters stood for! That made it difficult to reinforce the values that created the mantra in the first place.

IIIIIIIIIIIIIIIIIIIIIIIIIIIIIIIIIIIIIIIIIIIIIIIIIIIIIIIIIIIIIIIIIIIIIIIIIIIIIIIIIIIIIIIIIIIIIIIIIIIIIIIIIIIIIIIIIIIIIIIIIIIIIIIII

Once you have come up with the right phrase, it can be effective in managing your next blockbuster project, indoctrinating your newest employee, driving revenue initiatives, such as new client/contract acquisition—and managing expectations within them. I use my clients' Commander's Intents to guide the decisions I make on their behalf, to ensure that those decisions best reflect their true desires and fulfill their core values. So, too, should your employees.

Once you've got your CI firmly in place, we can talk about your You-ness—in other words, what makes you, you.

CHAPTER 8

Embracing Your You-ness

||||||||||||||||||||||||||||||

*You don't need to own anything to feel abundant,
although if you feel abundant consistently things will
almost certainly come to you.*
–ECKHART TOLLE

One of my favorite expressions is "Delegate everything but genius." This concept speaks to the heart of what I do, and why I do it. Take a moment to reflect on your own experience.

||||||||||||||||||||||||||||||||||||||||||||||||||||||||||||||||||||||||||||||||||||||||||||||||||||||||||||||||||||||||||

||||||||||||||||||||||||||||||||||||||||||||||||||||||||||||||||||||||||||||||||||||||||||||||||||||||||||||||||||

"What Makes You, YOU?"

What would your top three clients and your staff say, in three words (or sentences), is what makes you, you?

If you feel comfortable asking them, go for it! Then write down what they say.

||||||||||||||||||||||||||||||||||||||||||||||||||||||||||||||||||||||||||||||||||||||||||||||||||||||||||||||||||

Ask yourself, why did you become an entrepreneur? Why did you decide to choose this path when there are so many others to select? Why did you opt for the road less traveled? It's certainly not because it's easy!

Chances are, you chose this life because you believe you have something special to offer. You have something of value to offer the world. You have something that no one else has, and you uniquely know how to do it—and to do it well.

It is your *genius* that makes you, YOU.

Defining Your Genius

Genius refers to your unique talents, the You-ness of you, the reason why your clients have sought you out and hired you. Only one person in the world has your You-ness: *you*.

My You-ness is why my clients have hired me, and this "genius" is not something I can delegate. It's not something I can train others to do for me. Only I can do it.

What's *your* genius? For some entrepreneurs, defining their genius is a piece of cake. You might know exactly what you're good at: it's why you went into business for yourself in the first place. You've had years of validation, people saying, "You're really good at _____," and you know on a cellular level that this is your thing.

For others, defining genius is not an easy step. Modesty or lack of confidence can cloud our thinking—we may not want to brag. Maybe, over the years, you've started to feel diminished, like maybe your special gift is not so special after all.

But everyone has a You-ness—and you need to embrace yours! Imagine you have died and you are looking down from twenty feet above the earth, and you're seeing your epitaph somewhere, whether it's on a gravestone or something else. What does it say?

Maybe you are a writer. The gravestone might say something about your unique way of always discovering the best words to describe a particular moment. Maybe you are a fitness instructor. Your epitaph might say that you knew how to inspire people to be their healthiest selves. If you're a designer, it might say something about your sensitivity to beauty, or your ability to bring beauty into the everyday.

Whatever that special thing might be—that thing that makes you *you*, that thing that you might be scared to say about yourself, but you want so badly to be true—more often than not, *that* is your You-ness.

Don't Rob Yourself of the Good Life

To understand which activities correspond to your genius, start by asking yourself the following question: on your Perfect Day, a day that left you feeling completely energized by the end, what would need to happen? What would you have done? What would you have experienced?

I asked this of a client who is a writer. She told me, "To feel really fulfilled, I would need to have produced a solid block of writing. For me this means writing a bare minimum of 2,000 words." For you, the answer might be going to a certain number of sales meetings, or making a certain amount of progress in developing the prototype of a new product.

In order to complete these tasks that only you can do, you need to delegate everything else. Some of my clients come up with reasons why they can't delegate certain things. They might say, "Oh it's just quicker for me just for me to do it myself."

To that I would say, "That's the worst response ever."

Why? Because there will be ten more times this year that that exact activity needs to be done, and because you have been doing it, and you have not been training someone else to, the task will not be done by the right person.

So what's the big deal?

The "big deal" is that refusing to delegate robs you of your lifestyle. It's the root cause of LDD. If you have a bunch of small, thirty-minute tasks start to build up during your Perfect Day, you are going to end your day not energized, not actualized, and not totally thrilled and excited about your achievements. Instead, you will find yourself saying, "I was stuck in the weeds all day with this nonsense admin task that Sally or John should know how to do."

There is a saying by renowned psychiatrist and author M. Scott Peck, "Until you value yourself, you won't value your time. Until you value your time, you'll do nothing with it."

While all of this talk of you-ness and delegation may seem like "duh" material, it is rarely implemented in the daily life of the entrepreneur. In fact, if you haven't read Peck's *The Road Less Traveled: A New Psychology of Love, Traditional Values and Spiritual Growth,* I highly recommend it. Peck describes a life path free of LDD. Choose it.

I have to remind myself of my genius often, especially in those moments when I am tempted to avoid delegating. This has also become my response to the person who says about a task they should be delegating, "Oh, it will just take me thirty minutes." You know what? In thirty minutes, you could have called three of your top clients and asked, "How can I serve you better?" I'm betting that's going to help your referral business a lot more than doing that thirty-minute admin task!

Again, we'll go into delegation in more depth in Chapter 11. For now, I want to focus on the link between fear and failure—and how to avoid it.

Avoid the Fear-to-Failure Pipeline

Most people are afraid to say what their genius might be because, well, it can be scary. Once they determine what their You-ness is, they then actually have to go out and pursue activities related to that.

And what if it doesn't end up working out for them? What if it doesn't bring them energy like it's supposed to?

Many people are scared because they are not fully embracing their unique You-ness. In some cases, they don't believe they have this genius to start with, while in others, they are afraid to claim what that genius is. Any number of things can stand in the way of finding and owning your genius.

Maybe you have experienced this. You set out with the best intentions to work on the something meaningful, but then life gets in the way. You end up choosing, instead, the most simplistic of activities that don't involve failure or pain. Those are the things that get done. And the things that typically don't get done are the things that involve risk, vulnerability, pain, fear, time, or serious effort. Millions of people fall into these patterns. They are mired in the drudgery of daily existence and they don't really know what else life has to offer.

These people have Lifestyle Deficit Disorder. They are stuck with endless to-do lists. They find most everything dull because they are not living life in their sweet spot. They are not writing their 2,000 words a day or, at the end of the day, getting a call from their agent saying, "Your book is sold."

It's not happening for them because they're not doing the right activities often enough.

Recalling mindset, I mentioned earlier how 90 percent of your long-term happiness is predicted not by external circumstances, but by the way your brain processes the world. Our brains are physiologically wired to see the negative, to notice what's wrong. Most business owners—and people in general—have "scarcity mindsets." This is a sure trap for feeling like you will never have enough, no matter how much you have. People with a scarcity mindset say (and believe) things like: "I can't trust someone to manage operations," "I can't afford to hire that key person that my business is missing," or the more subtle and unconscious, "I don't have the skills or the ambition I need to succeed."

That is what living in scarcity sounds like. The mindset of "never enough"—whether it's *never good enough, never enough money, never enough success*—might be a world view your brain is wired to point out to you, but it is one you need to kiss goodbye. When our mindset is one of scarcity, more often than not, it translates into scarcity in our real lives. Yep, you guessed it: scarcity = LDD.

What fuels failure for people with this mindset? *Fear.* They are actually afraid of success, and their fear leads them directly to failure. The fear-to-failure pipeline has been around for centuries, and unfortunately, it only goes one way.

Consider a mindset of abundance. If you feed "abundance" into your brain, it's going to process the world with a totally different mindset than if you feed it "scarcity." *Never enough* becomes *I have more than enough.* And if you focus on having more than enough—more than enough time, money, talent, love, and energy—the externals of your life will soon match up to these thoughts. Do you recall the exercises you did on gratitude? *This* is what changes mindset. *This* is what every man, woman, child, business owner, employee, or stay-at-home mom or dad consistently falls short on: *gratitude.*

On her website *The Best Brain Possible*, Debbie Hampton offers this insight: "Neuroplasticity is an 'umbrella term' referring to the ability of your brain to reorganize itself, both physically and functionally, throughout your life due to your environment, behavior, thinking, and emotions. The concept of neuroplasticity is not new and mentions of a malleable brain go all of the way back to the 1800s, but with the relatively recent capability to visually 'see' into the brain allowed by functional magnetic resonance imaging (fMRI), science has confirmed this incredible morphing ability of the brain."[6] Hampton, the experts at Happify, and other studies too numerous to cite suggest you *can* teach an old brain new tricks. This learning can lead to a mindset change and can help with overcoming the fear-to-failure pipeline of LDD.

Championing Your You-ness—and Protecting It from Attack

Sometimes, the act of reaching the next level is about rediscovering what was important in the first place. This is especially true for entrepreneurs and solopreneurs who may feel burned out, exhausted, and no longer energized by the

---

6   Hampton, Debbie. "Ten Fundamentals of Rewiring Your Brain." http://www.thebestbrainpossible.com/the-10-fundamentals-of-rewiring-your-brain/

work they're doing. What was the You-ness that got you fired up about starting your business? What's the thing you used to love to do?

Take Sean, who is a gifted carpenter. Nothing gives Sean greater pleasure than making a beautiful oak table, cutting and sanding the wood, leveling it, and putting on a rich finish. Five years ago, he started his own furniture business to give customers high-quality chairs, benches, and tables, but he faced early financial difficulties that drained a lot of the joy out of the process. He had a couple of early clients who were the kind of people who enjoy trouble for trouble's sake, and they gave him bad reviews, which had a negative impact on his business. Sean started to doubt his ability as a craftsman. Before long, it was a struggle to pick up a hand saw and get down to work.

Along the way, Sean forgot how good he is at what he does. He's a terrific carpenter but a horrible delegator; all the things he needed to do to grow his business were neglected because he refused to hire any employees. Unfortunately, the demands of owning his own business required him to pay attention to activities other than sawing and sanding wood—and in an ironic twist, his craftsmanship suffered from the stress. His chairs and tables were no longer the beautiful works of art they once had been.

What's the answer for someone like Sean? He needs to rediscover his You-ness and stay in that zone. He's a genius carpenter, but he really isn't interested in the other stuff. If Sean hires other people to take on the other parts of the business—the finances, customer satisfaction, etc.—then he can reinvest in what he does best: working with his hands.

Sean adopts a Commander's Intent: **Quality above all**. This offers a way to ensure that every piece of furniture he makes is of the highest quality. And once he delegates the other aspects of the business to people who can also achieve quality in their respective zones, he's finally free to give his all to those tables and chairs. Sean now has a filter—"Quality above all"—that guides his decision making; he delegates everything except the *Quality of the craftsmanship*. Quality craftsmanship is his You-ness.

Got Joy?

Once you really get going with these practices—setting your Commander's Intent, identifying and protecting your You-ness—you will move toward living in the space of your genius. Joy, clarity, and energy are yours for the taking.

An additional benefit of this is that you will become more self-aware. And because your self is not static but dynamic, this means becoming more aware of how you are evolving.

This knowledge will help you advance to the next phase of your genius.

And since the true focus of this book is financial, motivated by your desire to have a thriving business, you have to believe that the, joy, clarity, and self-awareness we seek *do* have a business by-product: *Increased revenue.* I've seen it time and time again. Try it, you might like it.

As you build an empire, you train yourself, over the course of ten to thirty years, to do something, be good at it, and make money from it.

But inevitably something happens: you change.

This is absolutely normal. People change! We morph into different beings with different value sets as we progress through life. You have children, you have different relationships, circumstances change, and all of these things affect who you are. If you are an entrepreneur, chances are your self-worth is tied to the business you've built. The difficult thing becomes seeing who you really are, beyond that—to really understand what it is that makes you tick.

I always go back to Sarah, the pie maker in Michael Gerber's seminal work, *The E-Myth*. The pie maker was compelled to open the bakery because she loved to bake. She had a real genius—her You-ness was that her pies were out of this world. But as she grew and changed and developed new interests and capabilities, she grew to hate baking pies.

She was working excruciatingly long hours for not much pay. Her business was exhausting rather than energizing her. Sarah was no longer the little girl who had learned to makes pies with her aunt.

But that wasn't necessarily a bad thing. She had grown beyond the original dream of making good pies; she had other things she wanted to do, bigger challenges she wanted to take on with her bakery. She adopted a CI of **Caring deeply and often**. Every choice she made for the business went through that filter: caring about the ingredients, the kitchen, the customers, and the employees. With this new, expanded CI, Sarah enlarged her You-ness to include a vision of opening three new All About Pies shops, making $270,000 in annual profits, and selling the business for $1 million in seven years.

As an entrepreneur, your skillset will grow. Over time, the things that bring you energy will change. The challenge becomes keeping up with knowing who you are—and who you are becoming—as you go through these changes.

My husband is a perfect example of this. He's an industrial engineer by training. He used to get his thrills from landing a bridge contract and building a bridge or building a huge material-handling system for a plant.

His You-ness was in talking to the plant managers and training them to run a job, picking the right vendors, and making them look like rock stars to their bosses so that they ended up getting promotions. When he figured this out, he morphed his focus from industrial engineering into leadership coaching in his field. Does he still love a project full of trusses, steel, and fabrication? Yes. But his engineering practice now offers more—and his career satisfaction has gone up accordingly.

In order to discern what your true genius is in the face of changing circumstances and evolving interests, you need to be able to do the hard, honest work of getting to know yourself. It takes a little bit of pain.

But it also takes time and space. It takes being disciplined enough to block out the time and space to reflect on those big questions. What do I really want? What is my You-ness? What brings me energy? What has changed and not changed about my answers to these questions?

Taking the time in your busy schedule to honor and think about some of those things—whether it's through coaching, mentoring, or meeting with your staff and having meaningful conversations—will ensure that you continue to evolve.

Most entrepreneurs don't ever stay in place. Most entrepreneurs evolve pretty quickly—they change stripes and come up with the next "new wheel." Being stuck will rob you of these opportunities to birth the next new iteration of yourself.

If you are still accustomed to looking at your time as disposable chunks of thirty minutes here and thirty minutes there, you are missing the bigger picture. The stakes are high. If you want to live that Perfect Day, you must rediscover your You-ness, embrace it, and fiercely defend it with all you've got. Only when you do this will you be able to make the most of your time.

||||||||||||||||||||||||||||||||||||||||||||||||||||||||||||||||||||||||||||||||||||||||||||||||||||||||||||||||||||||||||||||||

SUGGESTED EXERCISE:
Finding Your You-ness

1. Understanding Your Genius—Part 1:

    Imagine that you have died and are attending your memorial service. What are your loved ones and colleagues saying about you? Take a moment to brainstorm words, phrases, moments, and memories that people would share.

    a. Spend fifteen to twenty minutes writing a eulogy for yourself.

    b. Highlight or underline key words and phrases. Display this prominently in your home/office so you are always reminded of what your genius is.

2. Understanding Your Genius—Part 2:

a. Ask yourself: On your Perfect Day, what three tasks would you have accomplished? Write those tasks down.

3. Understanding Your Genius—Part 3:

a. Make a list of four to five attributes that make up your "genius." These are the qualities that make you special. These are the things that only you can bring to the table—the qualities that your clients seek when they hire you.

b. For each attribute, jot down all of the tasks that are affiliated with that attribute.

c. Look over your lists. Can you delegate any of the activities to someone else? Write "Yes" or "No" beside each activity. For help on how to answer this question, cross-reference with the tasks you jotted down in "Understanding Your Genius—Part 2." Do any of these tasks compare in importance to the three you identified?

d. Review your lists again. Make a new list filled with the tasks for which you wrote "Yes." These are the activities you should be delegating. Hold onto this list—you'll use it again in Chapter 11.

CHAPTER 9

Making the Most of Your Time

||||||||||||||||||||||||||||||

By changing nothing, nothing changes.
–TONY ROBBINS

As part of a series of labor reforms, French lawmakers in 2016 proposed legislation to make it illegal for companies to send work emails to employees after hours or on the weekends. This was a response to the increase in work-related stress that had been brought on by the onset of digital communications. The intent was to protect the private lives of workers. The law argued that people had the "right to disconnect."[7]

---

7   Mosbergen, Dominique. "French Legislation Suggests Employees Deserve the Right to Disconnect," The Huffington Post.: May 27, 2016.

As entrepreneurs, we are responsible for creating our own personal laws. We have the freedom to take charge of our focus and activities. The fact is, while email and social media have done wonders for the modern-day workforce, they have also caused work and life to bleed together. Being continually "plugged in" can make us feel overworked without necessarily making us feel more accomplished or productive.

‖‖‖

"No-email Fridays"

France seems to be leading the charge on work-life balance. In 2016, Olivier Mathiot, CEO of PriceMinister—an online marketplace headquartered in Paris—instituted a "no-email Fridays" policy to encourage employees to resort less to digital messaging and to communicate face-to-face instead.[8]

‖‖‖

---

http://www.huffingtonpost.com/entry/work-emails-france-labor-law_us_57455130e4b03ede4413515a

8   Schofield, Hugh. "The plan to ban work emails out of hours." *BBC Magazine*: May 11, 2016. http://www.bbc.com/news/magazine-36249647

In our 21st century lives, constant communication is only one in a series of adversaries that can burn us out and deplete us of our energy. The pressures to do more, to have more, and to run in the hamster wheel of the twenty-four-hour workday take a tremendous toll on our bodies and our minds. They leave us gasping for air and desperately longing to have more of that one thing that, unfortunately, we can't produce: time.

I guarantee you, no one's Perfect Day is a twenty-four-hour workday.

This is our modern-day dilemma. But how do we solve for it? Any entrepreneur knows this question well, and it continues to be a concern for anyone who has employees. According to a study on time management conducted by the Institute for Corporate Productivity (i4cp), 53 percent of 332 polled companies have a "somewhat high" or "high" level of concern about the time management skills of their employees, and 46 percent feel the same way about workers' delegation skills.

This is all the more reason to hire well. Specifically, it might be vital to hire a good personal assistant or a virtual assistant who can take some things off your plate while also contributing to your success. But more on that in a moment.

First I want to pose a question: *How do we solve for time being a limited resource?*

Changing the Activity Mindset

I've put a lot of thought into this question. I constantly wonder how we can make better use of our time. How can we create a meaningful shift in our behavior from what we are doing today to what we could be doing to increase wealth and productivity?

When I talk about the relationship between time management and quality of life, business owners intuitively know that I'm going to say, "You need to take more time off," or "You need to take more time for yourself." They also already know their response: "Well, I don't have any time to do XYZ."

I'm here to tell you that your claim is patently untrue. With a little bit of strategic planning, and some effort and discipline, it is possible to design your life—your time—in a way that maximally benefits you and energizes you *around* your business's needs. Understanding how to do this is an important step in having the lifestyle you've always wanted.

Troy Shuette of Elite Waste Disposal keeps LDD at bay by honoring a time and delegation system designed to support the Perfect Day Lifestyle. "As a business owner, I treasure freedom. The irony is most people in business for themselves have no freedom. By first honing a time system that showed me where my time was most valuable, I was able to focus and a develop what I call a 'Self-Managing Company.' My day to day business runs without me. Having created a framework around me that has empowered my employees to do their jobs, means I get do my job and only my job. This has brought me tremendous freedom. The right mindset, meaning I don't have to do it all to be successful, has been key to my business success."

How can this work for you? Start with the beginning of the year. Typically what happens in a given year is that people will sit down and say, "Okay, here's what business life looks like, Monday through Friday." They will look at the deadlines for taxes and quarterly reports and schedule personal matters around them. In making plans, they may also be guided by when their kids' school holidays are. They will look at those dates and say, "Okay, that week is spring break, so we'll take a vacation."

But what if it were possible to have a radically different paradigm? What if you took a radically different approach to designing your time? What if you started out your year and said, "Okay, so there are 365 days in a year consisting of fifty-two weeks of five traditional business days. This means there are 250 business days, minus some holidays, so that makes around 240 business days." Right off the bat, you already have what could be considered 125 non-business days. That means a full one-third of the year can be devoted to you, *not* your business.

The problem, of course, is that entrepreneurs—like most people in the 21st century—don't work that way. But that's the way life could be! The entrepreneur has to learn how to "turn it off" instead of always being on the go. Why? More revenue and less LDD. Is that a formula enticing enough to motivate what, at first, might seem like a grueling change in your work time habits?

In the next few sections, I will explain how I go about designing my time system. But it's important that you come up with something that works for you and make it your own—*and* that you indoctrinate your staff to the system. Then, once you do so, you have to stick to it and believe in what it can do for you.

Stepping off the cliff is an act of faith. You have to believe that your parachute is going to work. You have to believe that if you actually take more time off, you will be more productive, make more money, and have more energy.

And it's true. I've lived it.

Why We Need F.R.E.E. Days

Let's go back to the start of the year. What if you sat down on January 1 and said, "Okay, with just Saturdays, Sundays, and holidays I have 125 F.R.E.E. Days?" (That's an acronym we'll be talking about shortly.) And what if, on top of that, you decided you wanted to take one day off during the week?

Would that be a huge boost to your lifestyle? That would add an additional fifty-two days off per year, leaving you with nearly 180 days free each year. That's half the year!

I know what you're thinking: "No way. There is no way I can take this amount of time off." Change your brain. It won't happen immediately, but in time, you *can*. And there you have it: a great recipe for your two-to-three F.R.E.E. Days per week.

It might feel like a huge shock to your system if you were to say, "I'm going to take off Fridays, and I'm not going to do any work then, nor on Saturdays or Sundays." But what if you had a strict set of rules around what those days should look like? What if you decided that you wouldn't answer calls or have lunch with a potential client or browse new business card designs on the internet, or even do a single household chore? *That* is the spice.

Defining what your F.R.E.E days are (and aren't) is a crucial step in warding off Lifestyle Deficit Disorder. This ensures that you don't wake up one day, after you've sent your kids off to college, wondering, "Who the hell *am* I? What do I like to do?" You don't want to realize one day that you're age fifty or sixty and have only ever worked on your business.

Say that you've devoted your whole life to business, and you come to a point where you have to sell your business. What will you do then? Are you going to play golf? Well, you aren't so great at putting. Are you going to go fly-fishing? You don't even know if you like to fly-fish. So what can you do about this? The fact is, you don't have to spend a week fly-fishing in Bend, Oregon, to learn if you like it. Start doing it on Saturdays.

This mindset shift is really about starting with your life first. It's about asking yourself, "What do I want to do *personally*—that is, *for myself*—this year?" You need to think about things like trips you want to take, family time you want to spend, and maybe even new creative ventures.

The first step is to brainstorm what you want to do, write all those things out, and then plug them into your calendar—just as we did in Chapter 3. Only then do you figure out the business stuff and let those things fit around your priorities.

Here's a handy mnemonic you can use to help define what a F.R.E.E. Day is for you:

Friends and **F**amily time (or "**F**or you" time, to recharge!)

Random act of kindness (it only takes thirty seconds to offer one)

Experience new things; set out on an everyday kind of adventure

Express gratitude

A F.R.E.E. Day doesn't have to include all four components, but you can pick and choose which elements feel right to you. A F.R.E.E Day in January might look totally different from a F.R.E.E. Day in August. The hope is that, whatever you choose to do, it fills you with a sense of freedom. No matter which activities you choose to engage in, they should make you feel happy and fulfilled. Even if you just meander about, you do so with intention.

My F.R.E.E. Days file is actually a bag—a pretty large bag. It has items to be returned to the store, gift certificates to be spent—it's basically an all-encompassing bag of goodies. I can load it in my car or drag it fireside for a deep dive in all things fun and non-work-related. My stationery lives in the bag; when else do I have time for a thoughtful note of hello or thanks? Anything that will support me being in a place of gratitude, random acts of kindness, adventure, and time with friends and family goes into the bag.

How Admin Days Can Refresh You

One of the bonuses of effective time management is that, not only do you generate more time for yourself, but you also generate more energy. Energy is like the bonus prize you get when you "win" the time-system game.

In my personal experience, the best way to partition your time and get energized is to set aside days to take care of all your administrative duties and leave the rest of your time to focus on the things that give you energy: your genius.

What's key to being able to have those F.R.E.E. Days is implementing the rest of the time system effectively. Dan Sullivan, CEO and chief guru at The Strategic Coach—the wellspring in which I was entrepreneurially baptized more than fifteen years ago—suggests dividing your work time into "buffer" and "focus" days. For each calendar year, you should have a certain number of buffer—what I like to call Admin Days—and a certain number of focus—what I call Revenue Days. These make up your workdays.

If you are working four days a week, which I highly encourage all entrepreneurs to strive for, you should ideally strive for three Revenue Days and one Admin Day.

On your Admin Days, you do all the things you need to do to ensure your life and business will continue running smoothly. These would be the days you schedule your doctor's appointments, sign payroll checks, and look at the business P&L. These are the things that have to get done that other people can't do for you. Careful here—be 150 percent true to yourself when asking if others *can't* do it. If they can, delegate these items and watch your Admin to-do pile diminish.

Using Your Time to Help You Create Energy and Revenue

Revenue Days, on the other hand, are days that are filled with revenue-producing activities. On Revenue Days, you will focus only on activities that will generate revenue for your business.

To get started, you need to first ask: How can you drive revenue in your business, consistently, using your You-ness—your genius? What activities bring you energy within your business, but continually come last because you're too "busy" with your email inbox or answering customer requests? Is it closing a deal? Is it learning a new skill? Is it being a good leader? Is it hiring or firing that person you've needed to hire or fire? Think about those things that bring you energy when you are in high-leadership and high-productivity mode.

|||||||||||||||||||||||||||||||||||||||||||||||||||||||||||||||||||||||||||||||||||||||||||||||||||||||||||||||||||||

"Expanding Your Genius"

What new skills or capabilities would increase your value to your business and drive profitability? Make a list below.

_____

_____

_____

|||||||||||||||||||||||||||||||||||||||||||||||||||||||||||||||||||||||||||||||||||||||||||||||||||||||||||||||||||||

This is much more than just thinking about the bottom line. Making calls to top-level clients or new prospects might be revenue-producing, but might not be energy-generating. Think about where in your business something is coming alive or sparking, and where *you* come alive, using your You-ness and your genius. These are the areas you need to identity and devote yourself to on your Revenue Days—and nothing else.

Does signing a check for payroll bring you energy and revenue? No? Then don't do it on a Revenue Day. If it's not on the list of revenue-generating activities, don't do it. If it's not your genius, Just Say No.

If you follow these guidelines, you will be able to eliminate the burnout that comes with the high-intensity life of the entrepreneur. Notice the ratio: if you are working a four-day workweek—which is my goal for everyone—you are spending three of those days focused on activities that bring you money and more energy, and only one day tackling the things that don't. Your Admin Day is the day that sucks the energy out of you. It is the day you sign payroll. The day you get rid of termites. Your Revenue Days are the ones that fuel you and keep your business vibrant and alive.

Now, I would never tell anybody just trying this system out to have a three-to-one ratio of Revenue Days to Admin Days right off the bat. As with anything, it's important to start slow and take baby steps. Start with a ratio of two-to-two, or don't be ashamed of one-to-three. Just start *today*.

If you can successfully execute two Revenue Days—days during which 80 percent of your time is spent on money- and energy-generating activities—you are well on your way to overcoming LDD and recouping your powers. If your day goes from eight to five, 80 percent of that amounts to only seven hours!

It Takes a Village—and Some Organization

The key to success is to make sure everyone who works with you understands your time system. Your staff has to get on board. You need to clearly communicate when you are available to address administrative activities and when you are not. Then, of course, you have to follow through.

My Admin Day, for instance, is Tuesday. Each person on my staff knows this. They know they have to plan ahead because that is the only day they get to barrage me with all the things they're stuck on or need my help with.

This sounds a lot easier on paper than it is in practice. You've got to be really committed—and really, really disciplined, especially if you are an entrepreneur suffering from LDD. You're going to get off track, and when you do, you need to have a system in place to help you recover so you don't become completely derailed.

One helpful tip is to come up with a good filing system. When you get off track on a Revenue Day—and you see yourself going through your stack of paperwork, scrolling through your email inbox, or perusing your Facebook page (you know you do this!)—you have say, "Whoa there. Stop!" And then you must immediately put aside whatever those items were that are not part of your allowed Revenue Day activities.

I have a filing system that consists of a big Admin Day file and a big Revenue Day file. If John Doe wants to refer me to Sallie Mae—and he's sent me an email about it, and I've already contacted Sallie Mae and never heard back—I'll put that in my admin file. Then on an Admin Day, I whip out that file and I have gobs of things I can do.

It takes discipline in order to effectively live in this time system. You have to train yourself to realize that the majority of your admin activities are not as urgent as you might think them to be. No one is going to foreclose on you in two days. You don't have to pay that bill right this instance, or whatever the case may be. Put those items in your Admin Day file and tackle them on your Admin Day.

Few things are so pressing that, if they are not dealt with immediately, it will cause your entire life to topple down like a house of cards. On the other hand, the house of cards might fall if you don't pull out your admin file and work on those items on your Admin Day.

||||||||||||||||||||||||||||||||||||||||||||||||||||||||||||||||||||||||||||||||||||||||||||||||||||||||||||||||||||||||||||||||||||||

SUGGESTED EXERCISES
Exercise One: Designing Your F.R.E.E. Days

1. If you could retire tomorrow, what would you do with the rest of your life? Make a list of all the things you would do.
2. Review your list and, for each item, ask yourself if those are activities you could start doing this week. Mark those items "Now."
3. For the remaining items, ask yourself if those are items you could start doing this year. Mark those items "This Year."
4. Look at your calendar for the rest of the year. Schedule at least one activity from your list to start doing this weekend. Schedule at least five activities to start doing this year.

Exercise Two: Know What Gives You Energy and Generates Revenue

1. Make a list of all of the activities you are responsible for.
2. Go through each item on your list and, as you do so, ask yourself, "Does this activity give me energy?" Mark "Yes" or "No" for each.
3. Make a new list comprised of activities marked "Yes." Label this list "Revenue Day Activities."
4. Make another list comprised of activities marked "No." Label this list "Admin Day Activities."

CHAPTER 10
Mastering Your Productivity

||||||||||||||||||||||||||||||

Change before you have to.
–Jack Welch

When clients come to me overwhelmed by distractions and unable to focus on their Revenue Days, I give them this simple advice.

"Take a scalpel to your time."

When a surgeon uses a scalpel, they are specific, skilled, and exacting. They do not make mistakes—or if they do, there is often hell to pay. A scalpel can cut away what no longer serves you, slicing into it with cool, unemotional precision. That may sound brutal, but brutal is exactly what you must be if you want to be productive.

Before I took this radical approach to time management, I felt very much out of control. Despite the fact that I worked hard and was generally an organized person, I constantly felt like there were not enough hours in the day, or enough days in the week. My time felt very unintentional and purposeless. The feelings of helplessness and lack of control were like a disease.

Does this sound like you?

If it does, the good news is that implementing a system of time management will help you regain your sense of control. Imagine that you have been given a magical scalpel, and with it you can carve out your time in the most strategic parcels possible. More importantly, this scalpel will excise the disease of purposelessness from your life.

If you are ready to move toward the life you want, then I dare you—no, I *double-dog dare* you—to take this weekend and map out the rest of the year. Start small: block out all of next month. Then go to your staff and make sure they understand when your Energy and Admin Days are, which we discussed in Chapter 9.

In this chapter, I'll give you a few actionable tips and strategies for taking a scalpel to your time.

What are you waiting for?

Better yet, can you afford to wait?

If It Takes Less Than Two Minutes, Then Do It Now.

This is David Allen's famous "two-minute rule" from his bestselling book, *Getting Things Done.*

Many people get in the habit of putting things off that they could have done in two minutes or fewer. We stack our plates in the sink instead of washing them right after a meal; we say "I'll take the trash out later" or decide not to throw the wet clothes into the dryer. Then the dishes get forgotten (and crusty), the trash doesn't get taken out in time for the garbage truck to pick it up, and the clothes start to get moldy in the washing machine.

Wouldn't it be better to do these things in less than two minutes, before there are negative consequences to *not* doing them? Why not tidy up clutter in your workspace while it's still a few manageable items, before it becomes the Leaning Tower of Papers and a veritable disaster zone? And doesn't it make more sense to answer that email with one brief line before you have ten other emails in your inbox competing for your attention?

If a task takes fewer than two minutes to complete, follow David's rule and do it right now.

Can all your goals be accomplished in under two minutes? Obviously not. But *every goal can be started in two minutes or less.* That's the purpose behind this little rule. When you start a new habit, it should take under two minutes to do. That will help you stick to it until it becomes the new normal.

For the bigger, more-than-two-minute tasks, here are a couple of apps I've found helpful:

ASANA for tasking what can't be done in two minutes;

SLACK (track messaging and intra-firm communications, project by project) for inter-team messaging without getting sucked into your personal texts or emails during your focus hours.

For those of you who are Gmail users, select **'AUTO ADVANCE'** to automatically show the next email when you archive the current email. This helps you to keep to a zero-inbox policy and prevents you from reading emails multiple times.

I also maintain a zero-inbox policy through a separate email, which I call "my Zenbox," where my staff forwards emails that are urgent and/or need my attention by end of day. **SANEBOX**, the email management service, offers a similar gift: it sifts out the necessary email by super-sleuthing non-important email and sending it to an alternate folder that you can delegate staff to read—or you can view it later, say on an Admin Day.

Pomodoros are Your Best Friends

Say you have created your list of Energy and Admin Day activities. You have a corresponding filing system to help you get organized spatially. How do you actually go about ensuring that the Admin Day activities get done during their scheduled times?

One very effective tool I use often is the pomodoro. Developed by Francesco Cirillo, the Pomodoro Technique is a method for time management that helps users combat distraction and boost productivity. One pomodoro is a unit of time—typically twenty-five minutes—during which only one task can be done. After that, a short break is permitted, typically five minutes. Then, move on to another pomodoro for twenty-five minutes, followed by another short break. After three or four series of pomodoros, take a longer, twenty-five-minute break before repeating the process from the beginning. A kitchen timer (or perhaps a cell phone timer) is used to mark the start and stop of the work/break intervals.

Pomodoros are helpful for both Revenue and Admin Days. The system is a great way to protect your time from distractions. Scheduling short, intense sprints of productivity can help you bite off those projects that are important for both business and life. Even if you can't complete an entire project in one sitting, you are at least generating momentum, and that momentum gives you tremendous energy.

The pomodoro was developed in the 1980s, but its applicability has never been more relevant. In today's world, distractions abound—including those created by your cell phone. In today's social-media-saturated culture, sources of "noise" are more numerous—and more persistent—than ever before.

Silencing the Siren Song of Social Media

How often do you find yourself in the following scenario? You start your day off right—you wake up early, work out, eat breakfast, plan your day, and are at your desk, ready to go, by seven a.m. You get to work and start to make progress on a project, when you realize you need to confirm dinner plans with a client. You email the client and start to look up the restaurant where you'll eat. There are some interesting items on the menu you aren't familiar with, so you look those up. Along the way, you chance upon an article on sustainable fishing and decide to post it on social media. When you sign on to social media, you start seeing other interesting things your friends have posted. Pretty soon, two hours have passed, and all you've done is peruse articles on Facebook and Twitter.

Even if you use pomodoros, you may still get caught up with distractions. The difference, however, is you can ensure that at least some of the important tasks of the day are completed. When you start to feel yourself getting pulled toward the siren call of Facebook, you set a pomodoro—twenty-five minutes of work, ten minutes of Facebook.

Lather, rinse, repeat.

At the end of four hours, you will have put in at least three hours toward your task. Not only is the completion of those tasks fruitful in itself, but the momentum you generate ensures multiplier effects.

Since I mentioned the biggest time suck of all them all, Facebook, let's chat about social media. The best advice I can give you is this: "Just Say No." Set times in the day that you can dial in and get your fix, but don't let the social media siren pull you away from what you really want. You don't need to share with your lead staff manager all that you learned about Suzie Smith's daughter's Student of the Month award, do you? Do you think your kids care about the political rants published by your 500 "close" friends and family? No, they don't. So don't do it.

Will your spouse care that you saw the cutest picture of a dog snuggling a kitten? Or will they care that you connected in a meaningful way with a human being today? A staffer or a random passerby does not give a flip that you liked ten posts on FB. Just say no and set a "no social media zone" to keep your productivity high.

||||||||||||||||||||||||||||||||||||||||||||||||||||||||||||||||||||||||||||||||||||||||||||||||||||||||||||||||||||||||||||||||||||||||||||||

Staying Focused with StayFocused

StayFocused is a Chrome extension that tracks and limits the time you are allowed to spend on "time-wasting websites" like Facebook. The tool is ultra-customizable—choose which websites (or specific pages) to block, how long to block them, etc. Whether Facebook or Twitter is your poison, or even if it's some other site, StayFocused helps deliver the antidote before the damage is done.

Alok Bhardwaj, the founder of Hidden Reflex, a software and web application product startup, says he starts his day by doing the least desirable task first.[9]

---

9   Insider, Kevin Smith Business. "13 tech leaders reveal their favourite productivity hacks to help you get more done." Financial Post. http://business.financialpost.com/fp-tech-desk/13-tech-leaders-reveal-their-favourite-productivity-hacks-to-help-you-get-more-done?__lsa=566d-27b3.

Bhardwaj offers six tips for how he gets things done. It all starts with doing the thing you don't want to do first:

1. Do least desirable tasks first thing in the morning. Try to work 2-3 hours straight on getting stuff done first thing in thing in the morning, before email or anything else.
2. Do not read any news, anything similar while working.
3. Workspace is for work only.
4. Daily to-do list of 3-5 things you MUST get done.
5. Don't try to do too much, don't try to optimize too much, delegate, stay focused on the big picture.
6. Exercise, meditate everyday.

CHAPTER 11

The Liberating Power of Delegation

||||||||||||||||||||||||||||||

No person will make a great business who wants to do it all himself or get all the credit.

–ANDREW CARNEGIE

A ndrew Carnegie's life was a true "rags to riches" story. He was Scottish born and immigrated to the United States with his very poor parents in 1848. Carnegie started work as a telegrapher and, by 1899, he owned over 25 percent of American steel production. He knew how to hustle to get what he wanted. By 1902, he was the richest man in the world.

Once he found success, he became a master delegator. His tombstone reflects this and reads, "Here lies a man who knew how to enlist the service of better men than himself."

He once told a friend who told him that he got to work at seven in the morning: "You must be a lazy man if it takes you ten hours to do a day's work. What I do is get good men and I never give them orders. My directions do not go beyond suggestions. Here in the morning I get reports from them. Within an hour I have disposed of everything, sent out all my suggestions, the day's work done, and I am ready to go out and enjoy myself."

There was no Lifestyle Deficit Disorder for Mr. Carnegie. The man knew how to delegate—and how to make every day his Perfect Day.

The Faith Factor

The problem with delegating is that it requires people to relinquish control of every little task in their lives. That is no easy adjustment, especially for control freaks. And more than likely, if you are an entrepreneur—especially if you are one who suffers from Lifestyle Deficit Disorder—you are a control freak. If you're anything like I was, you are a control freak in denial.

The irony, of course, is that people who are the most obsessed with control often feel like their lives are out of control! Naturally, the ones who desperately need to let go are the ones who have the hardest time doing so. But if they just took a leap of faith, they would see that delegating gives them infinitely more energy and freedom.

Chris Eller is an engineer and developer in Asheville, North Carolina. He's also an entrepreneur, the founder and president of Civil Design Concepts, PA. "Having a place to go that is an 'Execution-Free Zone' allows me to stay focused on what brings me energy. It allows me to step away from my team and empower them to do the tasks that I'm not designed to do. This, ultimately, energizes me so that, at the end of a day, I am my best me." Chris shared this with me when I asked what single best practice brings him closer to a Perfect Day Lifestyle—how *he* wards off LDD on a weekly basis. This is how he relinquishes control and stays on track.

The big question for me is, how do you "un-freak" a control freak? How do you teach people to do life differently? Maybe you are reading this and you have been convinced that you need to let go and hand off that thirty-minute task, but you don't know exactly how to break yourself of the bad habit of wanting to do it all yourself.

If this is you, the first thing you need to get a hold of is a little bit of faith. There is always a faith component required when you install new habits, particularly if you haven't yet seen the rewards. You need to believe that your efforts matter because *you* matter and your time matters.

The perfect example of what a little bit of faith can do is my husband. Once upon a time, he used to be someone who was a total workaholic. He worked nonstop and believed that it was the key to his success. But then he saw my business partner and me taking one day off a week. After a few months, our business actually skyrocketed—and so did our energy levels and our work-life enjoyment. I was procuring clients while side-court at Wimbledon, climbing in Russia, sailing from Charleston to Bermuda (I beat Stephen Colbert in a boat of women, much to his chagrin!) and then some.

My husband saw that time off could be beneficial and he became a believer in our methods. In his case, he didn't have to do the faith exercise, because he saw the proof! For you— well, I'm guessing you've invested several hours getting to Chapter 11 of this book, so why don't you try taking off next Tuesday? That's another double dog dare.

I strongly encourage taking the faith exercise. They say it takes twenty-one days to make (or break) any habit—good or bad. That's only three weeks. And if we're talking about taking just one day a week off, we're really only talking about three days. What do you have to lose in three days? Use those three days to practice delegating. You'll be surprised what your staff steps up to do now that you've passed the baton and aren't around to do whatever it is you shouldn't be doing.

I can guarantee that, if you can be disciplined enough to do this for three weeks, there is no way you will say that your lifestyle gains *haven't* improved by the end of it. You will have already had measurable success toward overcoming Lifestyle Deficit Disorder.

You will have clarity. You will have energy. People will treat you differently. Your staff will treat you differently. Your clients will treat you differently. Most importantly, you will start to see yourself differently.

In Chris Eller's case, he's taken delegation and un-freaking his inner control freak to a whole new level. He changed his physical environment and his mindset to support creative think time, unfazed by the daunting thought of execution. All to be delegated *later.*

Take the three-week challenge. Then, like Chris, perhaps you'll be ready to consider more.

How Your Commander's Intent Plays into Delegation

When you delegate tasks to your employees or vendors, you need three things:

1. trust of competency

2. trust of values
3. a shared language

All three of these equate to knowing, understanding, eating, sleeping, and breathing your Commander's Intent. If you trust in the competency and values of your employee or vendor to honor and fulfill your own CI—and if you are speaking the same language—then you can rest easy that you've delegated each task to the right person who shares your vision and will work with you to transform it into reality. These people buy into your Perfect Day.

The same is true for delegating your finances. Whether it's your bookkeeping and payroll, your tax return, or your investments and financial planning, once you've set a CI, you can delegate the non-core-competency tasks. Why? Because you can now trust that the staff and vendors to whom you are delegating tasks are "knighted" with the responsibility of carrying out your CI. They will know how to handle matters in your absence because they know what your expectations are. Set a clear and acceptable CI with each project you delegate, and ensure that the person executing knows you empower them to act on your behalf to carry out the task at hand.

Not so easy, right? I get it. But I want you to try it. This practice of reminding and indoctrinating staff and other professionals actually makes the hiring and firing process much more clear. If you are serious about curing your LDD, aim for utmost clarity between you and the people you entrust with these tasks. This clarity is paramount to LDD "remission."

Of course, you know the tasks you delegate are your "non-You-ness" tasks, responsibilities that do not require your own unique brand of genius or the magic spark that ignites your You-ness. Not only can you delegate these items on your business To Do list—you *must*. This will not only cure you of LDD, it will free you up to focus your time and talent as you refocus your attention on fashioning your Perfect Day.

||||||||||||||||||||||||||||||||||||||||||||||||||||||||||||||||||||||||||||||||||||||||||||||||||||||||||||||||

SUGGESTED EXERCISES:
Make a List of Tasks to Delegate

1. <u>Learning to Delegate</u>
   a. Make a list of tasks and activities you do on a weekly basis.
   b. Look over your list. Can you delegate any of the activities to someone else? Write "Yes" or "No" beside each activity.

c.   Review your list again. Make a new list filled with the tasks for which you wrote "Yes." This is the list of activities you should be delegating.

d.   Take out the list you made at the end of Chapter 9. Add these tasks for a complete list of tasks you should be delegating.

||||||||||||||||||||||||||

PART FIVE
In Conclusion: The Lasting Power of Relationships

||||||||||||||||||||||||||

I define connection as the energy that exists between people when they feel seen, heard, and valued; when they can give and receive without judgment; and when they derive sustenance and strength from the relationship.

—BRENÉ BROWN

CHAPTER 12

The Enduring Power of Relationships

||||||||||||||||||||||||||||||||

If you want to go fast, go alone.
If you want to go far, go with others.
–African Proverb

Let's take a moment to envision your Perfect Day.

Thanks to the exercises you completed earlier in this book, you have a good sense of what that day looks like for you. You know what you're doing and who you're with; you're engaged in activities that energize you and maximize your You-ness. You also know which tasks you *won't* be doing: the To-Do-list items and responsibilities you've delegated to the right people on your team, which has freed you to do the things you love the most.

Here's a question for you: did financial planning make the cut?

If you're like most of the people I work with, the answer is no. Even when I have clients who enjoy an active role in their own finances, granular financial planning work tends *not* to be a part of their Perfect Day. If this is true for you, you'll need to delegate this task, too.

I struggled about inclusion of this piece in the book. Then I realized my clients value the "barbell" aspect of what I bring to the table: my degree and formal training are my financial expertise, but human development and entrepreneurial happiness are my passion. So this section made the cut.

Today, there is no shortage of options when it comes to financial planning. Of course, if you're like the rest of us recovering from Lifestyle Deficit Disorder, "no shortage of options" may set off alarm bells. With a profusion of options, how do you wade through them all without retriggering your LDD, the part of your brain that lights up every time a new text message comes in? And more importantly: how do you know you're choosing the right option?

In a Wall-Street era riddled with conflicts of interest, delegating financial planning and investment management is not geared for the consumer's success. So what to do? DIY or delegate?

Financial Planning in the Era of Robo-Advising

There are immense benefits to finding a good financial advisor and cultivating a relationship with him or her. But even advisors need to acknowledge that, in this day and age, with all that technology has made possible, the traditional wealth manager is not the only option.

Robo-advisors started proliferating in the market about two years ago. They promise convenience and low to no fees. As a result, they present an alluring option for many investors and entrepreneurs, especially those who have become disenchanted with "do it yourself" investing. If you are currently choosing the DIY option and managing your own investments, I urge you to stop. The robo option may be a gateway for future years of hiring a competent, fee-only advisor. But it's only a start.

Investors and entrepreneurs are a savvy bunch—they're conscious of fees, they shop for vendors, and in general, they like to get the best value for what they're paying. Many of the needs of this group can be met by robo-advisors, and this is evidenced by the growth in the robo market.

While it may be tempting to delegate all financial planning services to a robo-advisor, there are some drawbacks to that option that bear considering. Robo-advisors may fill a niche within the market, and yes, managing costs is important, but these factors do not paint the complete picture.

The entrepreneur at the outset might be saying, "I want to cut my fees. I want to cut my costs." And in going to a robo-advisor, yes, they are going to do that. However, these advisors aren't designed or equipped to look at the bigger questions: What is your Commander's Intent? What are your core assets? What is your You-ness? How do you define your Perfect Day? Where is the best place for the next dollar you save or spend?

Let me give you an example. I have a client, George, who wanted a financial plan based on the following parameters: How much do I need to save in order to retire at age sixty and withdraw (a dollar amount) from my portfolio?

George did not have the cash flow or the liquidity to retire at that time, so the first steps of building his plan were to start devising a way to get more income. George and his wife, Ann, engaged in the Perfect Day Pyramid and created a Commander's Intent that was officially "The Freedom to Choose." Honoring that mantra meant helping George build liquidity as opposed to having assets that were locked up in stock and a very complicated business that was super illiquid.

In my work with George and Ann, as I walked them through the Vision Focuser and Perfect Day Pyramid exercises, they realized they wanted more than just to retire at sixty. What George and Ann truly wanted was the *freedom to choose* to retire at age fifty-nine or sixty-three. The retirement/financial plan that resulted from this conversation had a CI of "Liquidity." Without liquidity, George and Ann wouldn't have the freedom to choose when to retire.

If they had gone to a robo-advisor, or another advisor who functioned in a static planning vacuum, they would have received a completely different plan. The robo-advisor would not have been able to capture all of the nuances of George and Ann's true desire. First, the computer-generated questionnaire or the voice on the other end of the line would have asked, "What's your goal?"

To which George would have replied, "I'd like to retire at sixty."

From there, the algorithm would crunch some numbers and come up with how much George and Ann needed to save until age sixty. The result might have been much different than the plan we came up with based on a CI of "Liquidity."

The thing to remember is that, when clients are asked, "What do you want?" the pat answer they give right off-the-bat does not always fully reflect what they truly want. Yes, they know they want to retire, but there's usually something else driving what they really, really want. Here's one thing I know from more than two decades of listening to clients describe their current financial problem: "the problem" is *never* the problem. I suspect this may be true for you, too, in all your relationships: staff, children, friends, or even your spouse.

Two years later, after we put the "Liquidity" CI into place, George scheduled a meeting with me. "I have this opportunity within my business to get stock or cash," he said. "What should I do?"

Without a firmly rooted, value-aligned CI, another advisor would probably have run a simple valuation and said, "You'd make more by taking the stock deal. Take the stock versus the cash."

The problem is, that wasn't his goal! Because he had delegated his financial planning to me, we were able to run his question through the Perfect Day Pyramid and decide what choice was most in keeping with George and Ann's CI. We determined that taking the stock deal was not optimal, so George went with the cash instead.

Here's what George has to say about their CI: "'The Freedom to Choose' has directed a plan for our future that we feel incredibly lucky to have executed. Who knew? It's really amazing—the things we were talking about four and five years ago have fallen into place as we embark on the next phase of our lives."

How is the Perfect Day Lifestyle working for Ann? "This year has been all we could have hoped for," she says. "We've been taking the time to travel and remembering to embrace the relationships most dear to us."

The lesson here? It matters who your advisor is. You need to find one who is in tune with the bigger picture, not just the short term. And while you might think you know what you want, more often than not, what you truly want is something more than what appears on the surface.

Full disclosure: I'm a big believer in personal financial consulting services, human-to-human contact, and a relationship that grows and deepens over time. But I *do* believe there is a place for robo-advisors. If you feel called to go in this direction, there are a number of things you need to understand to maximize your experience with a robo-advisor, to make sure you get the maximum benefit with the minimum risk. If you want more information, feel free to consult my e-book, *The Liberated Investor*, which goes into more depth on the topic. It's a twenty-minute read, and you can download it for free at: http://www.liberatedinvestor. com/.

The Secret Sauce of the Personal Relationship

The key to having a successful experience with a financial advisor lies in the personal relationship. But here's the trick: there is no easy formula to prescribe what will bring about a fruitful collaboration—though there *are* some key ingredients that tend to make a winning recipe.

I have often had clients come to me and say, "Oh, I'm unhappy with my broker because of the losses that I have. My returns haven't been very good." I would then look into the situation and find that this was indeed the case.

But what the client was really dissatisfied with goes deeper than mediocre investment returns. What they really want is something else. The issue is more than that their broker hasn't called them; it's that the broker doesn't know who they are. Don't get me wrong—returns are important, but so is an advisor who "gets you."

The broker doesn't know that the client's mother has just died and they are coming into an inheritance. They don't know that your daughter has recently completed chemo and has received a clean bill of health. They don't know what the client's goals in life are. They might be simply planning for you to retire at age sixty.

When we talk about the personal relationship, it's important to keep in mind that there has to be an investment in an initial process that might be uncomfortable. And that's the "Where's your wobble?" bit.

The wobble piece is when you really talk about core values. These core values have a direct impact on the client's money, even if they are not explicitly a financial consideration.

One example of this is religion. On more than one occasion, a client will chime in and say, "My faith is one of my important core values," while the client's spouse will say, "Faith is not one of mine." And, of course, it's okay to have different perspectives on this matter, but an understanding of such things is important. When one spouse dies and they didn't have the proper estate planning documents in place, I will have known that that individual was not a person of faith. Therefore, they shouldn't be leaving money to the church. These are nuances that robo-advisors are unable to capture, and they illustrate just why a personal relationship is so valuable.

Most people who flock to robo-advisors do so because of their super-low fees—it's simple and technologically easy. All of these things are great, and I think that the client may feel like it's serving their needs. But the problem is, after five years with a robo-advisor, you will not have developed a personal relationship with anyone who can help you build the lifestyle you want. These things don't just happen on an intake form.

What happens when there is a crisis or a difficult decision needs to be made on the fly? Only an advisor with whom you have a personal relationship, one who really understands your values and knows your circumstances, can help you take the most appropriate steps. When you receive an inheritance, for example, or are faced with the question of "Do you take the stock or do you take the cash?" —you might make the wrong decision. The stock might look more lucrative on paper, but going with that option might undermine your overall goals. Only an advisor who knows you and your core values can provide the appropriate guidance when you have to make important decisions.

Vulnerability Is the Key

Working through the Vision Focuser and Asset Inventory often reveals to the client, "Oh, those are my sweet spots. Those are the things I really like in life. And those aren't the things I have right now." This process brings them closer to those revelations.

When we go through the Gratitude Exercises, among the first responses I hear are something along the lines of: "I'm so thankful I have a great spouse;" "We just got back from three amazing weeks in Italy;" or "I just had an excellent check-up with the doctor—I'm so happy to have my health."

The things that evoke deep emotion—the "touchy-feely" parts of life—are typically what people are most grateful for. Gratitude lists are usually not littered with "I had my best quarter ever in the business." It might show up, but it won't likely make the top four of ten items.

Going into those deep, emotional places sort of shuts off the analytical part of the brain. And it really softens the heart. When we start to dive into gratitude, we go to all sorts of deep places and topics: cancer, death and dying, life goals, grandchildren, love. The conversation doesn't usually go to the checkbook.

It also, inevitably, makes them more vulnerable, and vulnerability can be uncomfortable. But I welcome vulnerability in my client relationships. The Gratitude Exercise opens the door for a more honest and intimate relationship. When I am closer to my clients, I can do a better job for them and they feel more contented and fulfilled from our work together. We're all focused on a common objective: curing them of LDD and putting them on a clear, wobble-less path to their Perfect Day.

This is why I love working closely with my clients, rather than handing them off to a robo-advisor or an algorithm. It's part of *my* Perfect Day to help you draw a map from where you are *now* to where you want to be on your own Perfect Day, taking into account your CI, your You-ness, your core assets, and the people and relationships you treasure the most.

That's really what it all boils down to, isn't it? The human relationships in our lives are at the heart of every Perfect Day Pyramid, because they are at the heart of our lives. And I've yet to find a robot who can talk about matters of the heart.

CHAPTER 13
A Lifetime of Perfect Days

||||||||||||||||||||||||||||||

It is not the mountain that we conquer, but ourselves.
—SIR EDMUND HILLARY

As you probably know by now, I love connecting with people. Personal relationships form the backbone of my work, my Perfect Day, and my You-ness. People are at the heart of what makes me tick.

The beauty of the personal relationship is that, not only do I get to know my clients really well—but they get to know me, too. They know what they're getting when they sign on with me because I routinely share with them my thoughts and perspectives. And that means *I* get to be vulnerable, too.

Have you ever experienced being vulnerable with existing and prospective clients or strategic business partners, friends, and family? Share who you are with the world! Let others know your Perfect Days and how they impact your business and your life.

I remember one conversation with a new client some time ago. "How did you hear about us?" I asked. She said she had read an article about how my daughter summited Mount Kilimanjaro on an expedition with She CLIMBS.

The article mentioned how I felt like one of my toughest climbs had been Mount Rainier. As it turned out, this particular woman lived out in Seattle! She told me, "It just resonated with me—I live near Rainier. I love Mount Rainier." She formed a connection with me that was based on something that was entirely non-financial and unrelated to my business.

What resonated with her, and maybe with others, too—especially in light of the theme of this book—is that success is not all about money. It's about living your life, it's about experiences, and it's about crafting a vibrant lifetime of Perfect Days. Show your employees, your family, and your business relationships that you've cured your LDD—show them how the PD lifestyle is now a part of your fabric. It's who you are.

Don't forget that money isn't everything. It is not the be-all and end-all. Energy, renewed passion for my business, relationships, and health rank higher—and those don't exist within an aimless fifty-to-sixty-hour workweek. Could I have a lot more money if I hadn't spent so much on crazy climbs in different countries all across the world (not to mention all the climbing gear)? Absolutely. Would my portfolio be fatter? Yes, it would. My argument with the time system, however, is that your business should be making *more* as a result of more rejuvenating trips and F.R.E.E. Days. I live it—and countless others do, too.

If someone comes to me looking for advice like, "You need to save more," they may be surprised when the first thing I tell them is, "You need to live more." The reasoning behind this is, if you live more, you will end up making more *and* saving more. You will be healthier overall—mentally and physically—and as a result, your medical bills will probably be a whole heck of a lot less because you are going out there, living life, engaging, and being healthy.

The trick to all of this is authenticity. That is why I share stories about my experiences and post photos from my travels rather than using stock photos taken from the web. I want people to understand who I am because that is an important building block in establishing a personal relationship.

Who am I? I am YOU—a recovering LDD-er, a mom, an entrepreneur, a mountain climber, a wife, a financial planner. I've had to slog through a bunch of awful days before I sat down and wrote out my Perfect Day, and I spent years of hard work and dedication to turn it into a reality. Give yourself this same permission, but don't waste even one more day avoiding the PD lifestyle path.

Work to Live, Don't Live to Work

To be liberated, you first need to get a sense of perspective. You're an ambitious entrepreneur—this means coming to terms with the fact that work is not everything.

Let me repeat that: Work is not everything.

Yes, work is what drives you. You've chosen to become an entrepreneur because you love your job—or at least you used to. These are all good things.

But, there is a "but." Work is not everything, and if you treat it that way, you will miss out on a lot. You might risk losing your relationships. You might risk not fulfilling your true potential. You will lose out on being able to lead the life you deserve.

Remember: *The irony is that we are so stunningly loyal to our businesses, but our businesses are seldom as loyal to us.*

You may end up successful, according to some social metrics—heck, you may end up filthy rich—but do all of these things amount to happiness? Is it worth the sacrifice of your family, your health, and your personal joy to devote everything you have—mind, body, and resources—to your work?

Most business owners and employees alike live to work and forget that it should be the opposite: they should be working to live, working to fund their *fun. Working to to fund a life of purpose and meaning.*

Do you have blinders on like so many of the people around you? Perhaps you are unaware that this approach is problematic. Most times, the root cause is pure and simple complacency. But more often than not, there may be a paralyzing sense of fear. Taking your eyes off your business and turning your gaze inward can be scary! Maybe you've forgotten what it means to really have fun and to dream.

Chances are, you *are* afraid, and you're suffering from some or all of the above. It's time to reflect on your life and what is important. The consequences of not doing so are dire. At stake are your relationships with your spouse, your children, your parents, your friends, and yes, the success of your business. At stake is your health and vitality. At stake is your joy.

You can't solve the problem until you first admit you have one. Be honest with yourself. Do you have Lifestyle

Deficit Disorder? And if so, in which parts of your life is this most pronounced?

Once you can answer these difficult questions and admit to yourself that you have a problem, you are more than halfway there.

When Every Day Is Your Perfect Day

A lifetime of Perfect Days is not easy to come by. It requires hard work and discipline to say "no" to the things that are constantly grabbing at your attention and resources and "yes" to the things that matter most.

Saying yes is not as easy as it seems. It requires courage and deep self-awareness to say "Yes!" to the things that are important, the things that fulfill us, the things that sustain us—to embrace your You-ness and do the things that propel you out of your comfort zone and force you to courageously embrace your gifts.

Throughout the pages of this book, we have dug deeply into what this all means and what the implications are for our daily lives and the decisions we make. In doing so, we've covered a plethora of strategies for crafting the Perfect Day.

Now it's time for a quick review, to ensure that you understand the components to curing LDD and sustaining a PD lifestyle.

1. **Write out what you're grateful for.**
2. **Inventory your assets and focus your vision.**
3. **Define your Perfect Day.**
4. **Craft a Commander's Intent to help you get there.**
5. **Embrace your You-ness, your genius.**
6. **Manage your time and bolster your productivity.**
7. **Delegate, delegate, delegate.**

That's it. Seven simple steps. Easy, right?

Of course it's not easy! If it were easy, you'd have done this years ago, and you wouldn't need this book!

But don't lose heart. As the Chinese philosopher Lao Tzu said, "A journey of a thousand miles begins with a single step." All you have to do today is take one step, TODAY.

I hope by now you have gone through this book, completed all of the exercises, and made big plans for your Perfect Day. Your eyes have been opened to your own case of LDD and you are seeking a better way. You want to live with purpose and a focused vision. You want to stop settling for a life that is rife with exhaustion, distractions, and half-lived days. You are ready to climb the mountain.

Now recognize you will need some help.

Climbing the Mountain to a Better Life

As anyone who's ever climbed a mountain knows, it is not one steady ascent to the top. Hardly! You go up and down and up again, hiking down twists and turns, dipping into valleys and climbing up peaks. You cross terrain that is difficult—even treacherous at times—and there are moments when you don't know how you'll make it to the top.

And then, buoyed by your fellow climbers—your sisters and brothers on the mountain—you keep going. You put one foot in front of the other and you climb.

Life is like that, too.

Like any climber, you need a strong support system in place to cheer you on, encourage you, and pick you up when you fall down or lose your way. You need real, rich relationships from which you can draw strength, comfort, and solidarity. None of us can do this alone.

At this point, you have a choice to make: Do you continue the rest of the journey on your own, or do you reach out to get some support? This is a critical question you should be asking.

The answer is going to differ from individual to individual. It depends greatly on your personal circumstances, your goals, and your current stage in your journey.

What I can say is this: if you have determined that you want to go all the way, and that to do so requires some support, that's great! It takes a lot of self-awareness to know when to reach out and benefit from the support and expertise of others.

Hiring the staff who will support your new PD lifestyle—and letting go of those who will not—might not be easy, but it needs to be done. Choosing advisors who support and understand your Commander's Intent as it relates to what they do for you is integral for more Perfect Days.

The right person is someone you can trust. It's someone who fundamentally understands who you are and what your values are, and who is committed to walking alongside you in bringing you closer to the lifestyle you've always wanted.

Business, tax, and investment strategies, while important, are a distant second to relationship building.

Money matters are serious and intimate. Finding the right employees and/or advisors is therefore an exercise in trust. You must be able to trust the person—both their expertise and character—and trust their process.

Now is the time to reach out. I encourage you to create a tribe in whatever way feels right to you. Reach out to other travelers on the mountain path, and reach out to guides or sherpas who are willing to shepherd you to the top of the mountain. These might include financial advisors, life coaches, business mentors—or an all-in-one, Perfect Day Engineer. The right partnership can be transformative, not simply for your material wealth, but for your lifestyle as a whole.

That Perfect Day is yours for the taking. All you have to do is take that first step. Then keep on climbing, surrounded by people who want to see you succeed.

This is the journey of a lifetime: learning to summit the Perfect Day.

To feel the warm sun on your face.

To be with the ones you love.

To know you have all the money you need to be happy.

To be flooded with purpose and joy.

This is what I want for you.

Happy climbing, my friend.

AFTERWORD

As I was midway through the process of writing this book, my life changed dramatically. My husband and I decided to get a divorce.

I've talked about how experience assets aren't always positive—sometimes the most difficult, painful experiences are the ones that shape us most. We learn from them, we grow, and we're forced to face the things that are truly important.

No one ever plans to get a divorce. My husband has supported me in countless ways, both personally and professionally. But the truth is that our marriage was no longer working for either of us. Our family CI, "We choose us and that which energizes us," was not being abided. And it took a heaping dose of honesty for us to be able to admit that and find a way through. Both Tony and I have had to accept with grace the long-term consequences of betraying a sacred

Commander's Intent. We embrace this change in our family structure and both agree that even today, we are now better parents—and better to one another.

I don't think it's a coincidence that, as I delved deeper into writing this book, I chose to authentically confront what wasn't working in my business and particularly in my marriage. The work I'm committed to do with my clients doesn't just bring them closer to their core values—it has also brought me closer to mine.

Defining our core assets will always reveal the truth, and that truth may be difficult to face. But you *must* face it. The separation from my husband came to a head as I was in the process of writing, preaching, and living my truth. The words I was putting on the page forced me to hold myself to account. I strive to be an authentic person, and writing this book brought me closer to what I needed to do for my family and myself. These are the moments when all the other stuff peels away and we're left with the truths at our very core.

Sometimes, those truths are hard. But this is when it is *crucial* that we are honest with ourselves. Every day, I ask myself: What is most important? What is my F.R.E.E. Day filled with? How can I ensure that LDD doesn't creep back into my life and poison my relationships and my freedom? Then I go through the process of the Perfect Day in my brain. I truly believe that, if we can answer these questions with honesty and truth, we can find our way to freedom. Our lives will have greater, deeper meaning than they ever have before.

We've all been through hardships, and we know what it's like to end something. Whether it's the end of a marriage, a friendship, or a business relationship, or even the death of a loved one, part of being human is saying goodbye. What I hope for you is that this book will challenge you to use those experiences as fodder for growth—as a way to get closer to your core values. It won't always be easy, but it's worth it. You're fighting for the ultimate prize: a life of meaning, freedom, and joy. Go get it.

Morgan James
Speakers Group

We connect Morgan James published
authors with live and online events
and audiences who will benefit
from their expertise.

Morgan James makes all of our titles available
through the Library for All Charity Organization.

www.LibraryForAll.org

Printed in the USA
CPSIA information can be obtained
at www.ICGtesting.com
JSHW022332140824
68134JS00019B/1447